D1196771

SONS OF NORWAY
TROLLHEIM LODGE NO. 511
BOX 632
ST. CLOUD, MN 56302

Received September 2018

FROM AMERICA TO NORWAY

Norwegian-American Immigrant Letters, 1838–1914

FROM
AMERICA
TO
NORWAY

NORWEGIAN-AMERICAN
IMMIGRANT LETTERS
1838-1914

VOLUME FOUR: INDEXES

EDITED AND TRANSLATED BY

Orm Øverland

Norwegian-American Historical Association
Distributed by the University of Minnesota Press
NORTHFIELD, MINNESOTA, 2018

Copyright 2018
Norwegian-American Historical Association
Northfield, Minn. 55057
www.naha.stolaf.edu

Distributed by the University of Minnesota Press
111 Third Avenue South, Suite 290
Minneapolis, Minn. 55401
www.upress.umn.edu

A Cataloging-in-Publication record for this book
is available from the Library of Congress.
ISBN 978-1-5179-0519-4

CONTENTS

FOREWORD

The fourth volume of *From America to Norway* concludes Orm Øverland's magisterial English edition of correspondence written by Norwegian immigrants in the United States and sent to Norway. Although primarily intended to provide indexes, this slender book is enriched with a concluding essay and a bibliography of other such letters published by the Norwegian-American Historical Association. Professor Øverland's essay draws attention to the importance assigned to the publication of correspondence by the founders of the Association. This has been a persistent theme throughout the years since the establishment of the organization in 1925.

It remains now only to thank Orm Øverland once again for making these riches available to contemporary readers in English. This took the love, devotion, erudition, and stamina of a dedicated scholar with a generous heart and a brave spirit. I thank as well Amy Boxrud and Ann Schroeder, who provided advice and support in the production of this volume.

Todd W. Nichol, Editor
Northfield, Minn.

INTRODUCTION

DISCOVERING IMMIGRANT LETTERS

AND

CREATING THE NORWEGIAN-AMERICAN HISTORICAL ASSOCIATION

Two stories, that of the making of the collection of immigrant letters in the Norwegian National Archives in Oslo and that of the creation of the Norwegian-American Historical Association (NAHA) at St. Olaf College in Northfield, Minnesota, in 1925 are so closely interwoven that it is difficult to tell the one without also telling the other.[1] The overlapping of the lists of key characters in these two stories will unavoidably lead to repetition if the stories are told separately. This introduction focuses on the existence of the immigrant letters, the growing realization of their importance, the many attempts to collect them and to find a way to organize a collection, the difficulties of funding a collection, and the decision to place the collection in Norway where the letters were sent.

The preparations for the centennial celebration of organized emigration from Norway to the United States in 1925 were widely publicized in the Norwegian language press in the United States and led to a heightened awareness of ethnicity as well as an increased interest in the history of immigration. The centennial was marked by large-scale public celebrations in Minneapolis and St. Paul.[2] A far more modestly attended event was the gathering of a few prominent Norwegian Americans in Northfield, a small Minnesota town south of the Twin Cities. They had responded to a printed invitation to discuss "The Proposed Society for the Preservation of Historical Relics and Records of Norwegian-American Pioneer and Cultural Life," and their decision to create a historical society had a more lasting impact on our understanding of Norwegian-American history and ethnic culture than the

---

1. An earlier Norwegian version of this essay, "Hvordan Riksarkivets amerikabrev samling ble til," is the introduction to Volume V of the Norwegian edition of these letters.

2. A fine study of the centenary celebrations is April R. Schultz, *Ethnicity on Parade: Inventing the Norwegian American through Celebration* (Amherst: University of Massachusetts Press, 1994).

parade and pageant in the Twin Cities.[3] The founding of the Norwegian-American Historical Association was born of the conviction shared by many prominent members of the immigrant community that important sources for the history of the Norwegian immigration to the United States would be lost if nothing was done to collect them, preserve them, translate them into English, and make them available to scholars.

This conviction was by no means new. No sooner had immigrants from Norway begun to arrive than individuals among them had advocated the organizing of a society for the collection and preservation of sources for a history of the migration. The earliest attempts to create such an organization occurred as early as the 1840s and 1850s.[4] In his first editorial in the Chicago newspaper *Skandinaven*, Knud Langeland spoke for the importance of creating a historical record: "No people can claim to be civilized unless it leaves behind testimonials to its history."[5] A fine study of early attempts to create a historical association, concluding with the founding of NAHA in 1925, is Lloyd Hustvedt's article "The Norwegian-American Historical Association and Its Antecedents."[6] In 1975 Kenneth O. Bjork and Odd S. Lovoll, the second and third NAHA editors, published an account of the founding and the first fifty years of the association.[7] No other single issue was so prominent in the minds and discussions of the founders of the association as the letters immigrants had sent to Norway, and no other group of sources proved so difficult to collect. Although these letters had been written in the United States, they would have to be sought in private homes in Norway, where historians had not previously regarded them as sources of interest for historical research.

In nineteenth- and early twentieth-century Norway, the authorities, conservative intellectuals, and members of the upper classes had negative

3. NAHA, Ole Edvart Rølvaag Papers, P584, Box 6, File 6. This invitation is dated July 24, 1925, and was enclosed in a letter from Kristian Prestgard to Ole E. Rølvaag dated August 17, 1925.

4. See Orm Øverland, "Bearing Historical Witness," in *The Western Home: A Literary History of Norwegian America* (Northfield, Minn.: Norwegian-American Historical Association, 1996), 69–76; and "History as a Prerequisite for an Ethnic Identity: The Roots of Organized Historical Research and Publishing among the Norwegian Americans," in Hans Storhaug, ed., *Norse Heritage – 1989 Yearbook* (Stavanger: Norwegian Emigration Center, 1989), 117–127.

5. Knud Langeland, *Skandinaven*, June 1, 1866. My translation.

6. Lloyd Hustvedt, "The Norwegian-American Historical Association and Its Antecedents" in *Americana Norvegica III*, ed. Sigmund Skard (Oslo: University of Oslo, 1971), 294–306.

7. Kenneth O. Bjork and Odd S. Lovoll, *The Norwegian-American Historical Association 1924–1975* (Northfield, Minn.: Norwegian-American Historical Association, 1975.)

views of emigration as well as of the emigrants themselves: emigration, in their view, tapped the homeland of its laborers and farmers. The dominant conservative attitude toward the immigrants was that those who had left no longer belonged to the nation. Consequently, there was no reason to be interested in them or their letters. An early expression of such a negative attitude toward emigration is the 1837 pamphlet translated by Gunnar J. Malmin as "Bishop Jacob Neumann's Word of Admonition to the Peasants" in the very first publication of the Norwegian-American Historical Association.[8] In such a social and ideological context, the letters from emigrants were an important alternative source of information; emigrants provided new ideas for common men and women simply because they described life in the United States.

Most letters the early immigrants sent to their former homes and neighborhoods did not advise others to follow. On the contrary, the early letter writers were careful to insist that they would not advise their readers one way or the other. Those at home receiving the letters would have to make up their own minds and be responsible for their own decisions. Indeed, writers often insisted that their readers would not benefit from emigration and that if they emigrated their motivation should be to benefit their children and not themselves. On the other hand, it goes without saying that immigrants who failed in their endeavors and lived miserable lives in the New World were not frequent letter writers. So most letters did tell of success, however moderate, and were clearly important in motivating many to leave and to direct them to where they should go to be among friends and relatives.[9]

Jacob Neumann was certainly aware that letters from the United States were circulating among the common people of his diocese. The first letter in the first volume of this edition was preserved because a local police officer had a copy made and sent it to the bishop in Bergen. Evidently the constable regarded it as a seditious document.[10] More liberally inclined intellectuals, however, regarded the letters as alternative sources of information for the common man. Thus Alexander Kielland in his novel *Fortuna* (1884) has a

8. Gunnar J. Malmin, trans., *Norwegian American Studies and Records 1* (Northfield, Minn.: Norwegian-American Historical Association, 1926), 95–109.

9. For a discussion of immigrant letters see my introduction, "Listening to the Voices in Immigrant Letters," in the first of these three volumes.

10. This letter, dated July 10, 1838, and written by Svein Knudsen Lothe to his brother at Aga in Hardanger, is discussed in my article "Religion and Church in Early Immigrant Letters: A Preliminary Investigation," in *Crossings: Norwegian-American Lutheranism as a Transatlantic Tradition*, ed. Todd W. Nichol (Northfield, Minn.: Norwegian-American Historical Association, 2003), 31–56.

lawyer with somewhat radical views explain that while the upper classes in Norway had stagnated, the lower classes were undergoing change because

> they read and reread the thousands of letters from the Norwegians in America that flow into the country every year. You see, this is a source of education that is superior to all newspapers and books, because here the people are for the first time taught by their own kind, in their own language and with reference to their own culture—the only one that an individual may truly understand.[11]

In 1925, another Norwegian writer, Hans Aanrud, introduced his review of the Norwegian edition of Ole E. Rølvaag's *Giants in the Earth* with some reflections on the immigrant letters, and Kristian Prestgard, editor of the Norwegian-American newspaper *Decorah-Posten*, used Aanrud's words to conclude a long editorial on the America letters: "They were in a manner of speaking the newspapers of their time—newspapers that spoke to them quite personally. They gave glimpses of other, greater and more difficult ways of life; they spoke of other struggles and conflicts than ours, other victories and other defeats. They gave visions and fed the imagination; there can be no doubt that they created greater ambitions."[12]

Historians on either side of the Atlantic, however, were only just beginning to take interest in the deeds and thoughts of common men and women when Prestgard wrote his editorial. The beginning interest among academic historians in the doings of uneducated peasants and laborers must be seen in the context of the new interest in social history in the early decades of the twentieth century. It may be noted that among the pioneers in American immigration history were three historians who had grown up in Scandinavian immigrant families: the Swedish American George Stephenson, the Danish American Marcus Lee Hansen, and the Norwegian American Theodore C. Blegen (1891–1969), who also has a central role in the story to follow. In Norway, Ingrid Semmingsen was the first prominent historian who studied emigration as a main area of research. It should be noted, however, that with few exceptions it was amateur historians who both created the Norwegian-American Historical Association with its archives at St. Olaf College in Northfield, Minnesota, and who initiated the collection of immigrant letters in Norway.

---

11. Alexander Kielland, *Fortuna*, Vol. 6 of *Samlede Verker* (Oslo: Gyldendal, 1949), 94–95.

12. Kristian Prestgard, *Decorah-Posten*, December 8, 1925; my translation. Prestgard had this editorial reprinted on a separate sheet as part of his information campaign for the new historical association.

This chapter of the story begins in Decorah, Iowa, home of Luther College as well as of *Decorah-Posten*, then one of the most influential of the Norwegian language newspapers, and the main character of this chapter is a young student, Gunnar J. Malmin (1903–2000), who graduated from the college in 1923.[13] That year his clergyman father, Rasmus Malmin, became a member of the Centennial Committee and we may assume that the planning of the coming celebrations as well as immigration history were conversation topics in the Malmin home where the main language was Norwegian. At Luther College, Gunnar Malmin's history professor was Knut Gjerset (1865–1936), the author of a two-volume *History of the Norwegian People* (1915) who was then completing another major work, his *History of Iceland*, to be published the following year. Gjerset was also involved in preparations for the centennial celebrations and was responsible for creating a collection of Norwegian and Norwegian-American artifacts for a planned exhibit in St. Paul, a collection that formed the beginnings of Vesterheim, the Norwegian-American museum in Decorah. Both Gunnar Malmin's history professor and his father were strong influences on the young student's interest in immigration history, but the more immediate influence on Malmin's decision to go to Norway to search for sources for the history of Norwegian emigration was his conversations with Theodore C. Blegen, then still in a junior position at the Minnesota Historical Society in St. Paul, just a few hours by train from Decorah. For some years, Blegen's major ambition had been to write a history of Norwegian immigration, and he was the first historian to realize the importance of the immigrant letters as sources for such a history. Indeed, his article "The America Letters," which appeared in the Minneapolis journal *The North Star* in February 1920, was most likely the first use of this well-established Norwegian term (*Amerikabrev*) in English. But Blegen saw no way of crossing the ocean for studies in Norway, and in conversations with the Luther College student he must have realized the young man's potential for research; it was Blegen who gave Malmin advice and guidance and helped him to get scholarships from both the Carnegie Institution and The American Scandinavian Foundation. When Malmin went to Norway in the summer of 1923 he was well prepared for his task. In the course of the fall and winter months he spent researching

---

13. Gunnar J. Malmin was interviewed for the oral history project at Pacific Lutheran University. See the Scandinavian Immigrant Experience Collection of oral histories at *plu.edu/ archives/sie/oral-history-collection/*.

in several public archives, libraries, and in some private homes, Malmin discovered a wealth of source material and created the foundation for the later research of Blegen, Semmingsen, and many others.

In Norway, Gunnar Malmin hunted for sources for a history that no one had previously told. His hunt took him to the university library in Oslo (now the Norwegian National Library) and the archives of government ministries as well as the four county archives (*Statsarkiv*) in Oslo, Hamar, Bergen, and Trondheim, and the National Archives (*Riksarkivet*) in Oslo.[14] Such institutions were rarely visited by people of his age, and in a brief article, "Paa Jagt i de norske Arkiver" ("Hunting in the Norwegian Archives") in the Minneapolis *Familiens Magasin* ("The Family Magazine"), Malmin writes entertainingly about his experience of archival research:

> Here in the National Archives I would often happen to sit at the same table with some of the country's most prominent historians. I really enjoyed looking at these old veterans who in their appearance and demeanor reminded me of the legendary "absent-minded professor" surrounded by all manner of strange documents, records, and journals! This is quite strenuous work. The handwriting is often so minute or obscure that you have to make use of a magnifying glass. And the dust is all pervasive! Hands, face, and clothes all get dusty and your collar cannot long remain clean when you are engaged in such work! At the end of the day your eyes and your head are exhausted and you are dusty from top to toe. But it is great fun. You can never know what manner of strange things you may happen to come across. In the midst of all the mess there may perhaps be a little letter, a few words that could change our understanding of history.

Although the archives and libraries he sought were of course well organized, they were not organized for the search that Malmin was engaged in. "The card catalogues were of no help," he writes, and explains that he had to search in the Parliamentary Proceedings (*Stortingsforhandlingerne*) "and other printed documents to find references. Old newspapers were also helpful."[15]

---

14. These repositories are specifically noted in Malmin's typewritten report to the Carnegie Institution.

15. Gunnar J. Malmin, "Paa Jagt i de norske Arkiver," *Familiens Magasin* (No. 12, September–October 1925), 13. This and following quotations from this article are in my translation.

Malmin's progress may be traced in six letters he sent to Knut Gjerset.[16] More adventurous than more mature and established scholars, Gunnar Malmin actually worked his way across the Atlantic, arriving in Oslo (then Christiania) by ship on July 16 in the company of a group of Norwegian Americans visiting their home region of Valdres. After taking an active part in their celebrations in Vestre Slidre as an organist, he went on to visit family in Vågå in the valley of Gudbrandsdalen, stopping in Lillehammer to see the large outdoor museum collections at Maihaugen. Back in Oslo he seems to have been as interested in music as in the history of emigration and he wrote enthusiastically about his meeting with the musicologist Ole Mørk Sandvik, promising to send Sandvik's two-volume history of music in Norway to the Luther library.[17] Malmin wrote this first letter on August 7, only a few days after his visits to Valdres and Gudbrandsdalen, yet he was already hard at work and had established good relations with a senior archivist (*førstearkivar*) at the National Archives, Christopher Brinchmann:

> Needless to say, I am enjoying my trip and my stay here immensely, and I again wish to thank you most sincerely for the part you have played in getting me here, as well as for the many ways in which you have helped me in my work while at school. However, the best way for me to show my appreciation will be to do satisfactory work and make the best use of my stay here, and that is what I am earnestly trying to do.

Indeed, he was then also at work in the archives of the Ministry for Social Affairs (*Socialdepartementet*) and already had an idea for an article that Gjerset had urged him to write—"The Attitude of the Norwegian Government towards the Emigrant"—but he realized that he "may find some other topic that would be of greater interest." On September 1 he had taken part in the annual matriculation ceremony at the University (at this time there was only one in Norway) but he evidently did not find time to attend any courses.[18] When he wrote again on October 22 he reported that he was "now practically through" with his work in Norway and was "leaving tonight on my way to Stockholm." He seems to have been rather

---

16. Five letters dated Christiania, Norway, August 7, October 22, and December 5, 1923, and January 15, 1924, and one dated Copenhagen, March 29, 1924, are in the Luther College archives, Knut Gjerset Papers, Box 1, 28:2. A sixth dated Rome, April 19, 1924, is in the Knut Gjerset Papers in the NAHA archives, P683, Box 1, File 2. Malmin wrote in English to Gjerset. Copies of the letters in the Luther College Archives were sent to me by Professor Øyvind Gulliksen.

17. *Norges musikkhistorie*, edited by Ole Mørk Sandvik and Gerhard Schjelderup, was published in two volumes in 1921.

18. He did not write about his matriculation until December 5, 1923.

discouraged and wrote that "there is very little material in the official archives here" and that the little he had found was "of no great interest or value." The most interesting material he discovered seems to have been among the Quakers in Stavanger where he had established good relations with the leader of the congregation, Thorstein Bryne. By this time, however, he had realized that the most interesting source material to be found in Norway were the letters from immigrants. These letters had been read carefully when they were first received,

> But, when the first excitement had passed over, no one cared very much about keeping the letters. Or perhaps they were kept as long as "the old folks" were alive; they were probably packed away in a box in the attic, or in a drawer. But when the younger generation grew up and started "house-cleaning" the old letters probably went to feed the bonfire. A lot of valuable material has been lost in this way. Some of the letters, even from the very earliest period of emigration, could still be found, scattered around in private homes in the country, I am sure. Especially the *bondegaarder* [farms], where the same family still lives, have such old letters. How valuable a collection of such old letters would be! It would not be an easy matter to collect this material, but something ought to be done.

Malmin had also been at the home office of Nordmands-Forbundet, an association of Norwegians and descendants of Norwegians abroad, and had spoken with the secretary general, Sigurd Folkestad, but in spite of their interest he concluded that they were "not at present able to start such a collection."

Malmin's visits to Stockholm and Uppsala in November and Copenhagen in March did not lead to any interesting discoveries. As he wrote on December 5, "The sum and substance of my work in Sweden, then, is: I wasted a lot of time for a large number of busy men, and found next to nothing. Indeed by this time he seems to have been rather discouraged at least as far as his archival research was concerned:

> The archivists and librarians I have spoken with have all looked very much puzzled when I have explained my mission. The material which I have found has not, strictly speaking, been *archive material*, as it is not kept in any official archive. If Dr. Jameson had known this, a Fellowship would hardly have been given for this purpose.

But as he continued to report on what he had actually achieved, it is clear that he was not as discouraged as this posture may suggest. He writes of his plan to use the material he has found in a history he thinks he may call

"A Hundred Years of Norwegian Emigration," based on his research in the Parliamentary Proceedings, the archives of the Ministry for Social Affairs (*Sosialdepartementet*), the Church Ministry, and the newspaper collections in the university library. It is clear that this young and inexperienced scholar had by this time located and studied some of the central sources for much of the early work of NAHA, for instance letters by Johan R. Reiersen and Elise Wærenskjold, and interesting documents concerning the establishment of an immigrant church. He doubted that he would ever publish a study using this material but we who have the advantage of hindsight know that he was right in his modest assumption that "it will at least be of interest and help for historians who may work with this subject in the future."

By the time he wrote again from Christiania on January 15, 1924, he was far more optimistic. He now believed he had sufficient material for the master's thesis he was planning to write at the University of Illinois at Urbana and asked Gjerset "to write a few lines in support of my application." It seems that his discovery of how much relevant material could be found in the old newspapers in the university library had fired his imagination:

> I have been surprised to find what a wealth of material there really is, not only on emigration in itself, but also regarding the history of our people in America. There are three kinds of material: 1) Reports as to the departure of emigrant ships, or reports as to the number of emigrants from some specific district, with a few remarks as to how sad it is to see them leave, etc. 2) articles as to the causes of emigration, and how these causes can be removed, and 3) letters from Norwegians in America, as to how they are getting along over there, and, in most cases, advising friends and relatives to come over, too....

> I am finding the work more and more interesting as I go along. I only wish that I had had more experience in this sort of work before, because I am often quite puzzled as to the best way of proceeding. But I am doing what I can with it. It's a slow job working with the newspaper material, as most of the newspapers have no index, so I have to page through everything. It seems strange that no one has gone through this material before, and yet such, I believe, is the case.

When he wrote from Copenhagen on March 29 he felt he had completed the work he had set out to do and he seems to have been quite satisfied with what he achieved:

> As you undoubtedly already understand, the idea of the Carnegie Institution in carrying on these investigations in all European archives is to locate all material that can throw any light on American History. One

becomes quite amazed to find how much good, interesting and valuable material there really is, even in such comparatively small and insignificant countries as Norway, Sweden, and Denmark. My work over here, then, is to find all such material, describe it carefully, and, of course, bring out what appears to be the truly valuable material. I have often felt that I am altogether too young and inexperienced for this kind of work, but I have done my best with it, and have certainly found it very interesting.

About a week after he wrote this letter he set out on an excursion through Germany, Italy, Switzerland, and France before he returned to Norway by the end of May and then went home in August.

When he wrote to Gjerset from Rome he told him that he would like to place the material he had collected in the library of Luther College.[19] The impressive nature of this material may be seen in the two reports he wrote about his findings. One is the forty-nine-page typewritten, detailed report he submitted to the Carnegie Institution in the spring of his homecoming. His other report is, we may say, addressed to all Norwegian Americans in that it was published in a series of nineteen installments in *Decorah-Posten* that began on November 14, 1924, and concluded March 27, 1925.[20] The title for the series of articles is, in translation, "The Norwegian Land-Taking in the U.S.: Documents, Letters, Reports, and other Information on the earliest Norwegian Emigration and the First Pioneer Period in America."[21] He begins his first installment with a rather modest statement of purpose: "My aim with this series is not to give a thorough historical account of the Norwegian emigration but merely to present some of the best sources I have found in my studies of this topic. It will be sufficient to let the documents speak for themselves with only a few remarks to give the reader a reasonably cohesive account. However, it may be best to begin with an introductory or explanatory chapter as a sort of historical background for the series." Installments II to V are concerned with the first group of emigrants from Stavanger in 1825 and with sources to be found among the Quakers in that city. The next three installments are titled "Official Documents" and are concerned with what he had discovered in various ministries as well as in

19. April 19, 1924. See note 16 above.

20. The report as well as clippings of the articles in *Decorah-Posten* are in NAHA, Gunnar J. Malmin Papers, P235. All quotations are in my translation.

21. Land-Taking is my translation of "*Landnám*," an Old Norse word that was originally used in reference to the medieval settling of Iceland in the early tenth century. Ole E. Rølvaag used the word *landnám* in his dedication to the first volume of the Norwegian edition of *Giants in the Earth*, published as *I de dage* in Oslo in 1924, where Malmin probably saw it and adopted the phrase for his own use.

the National Archives. Many of the nineteen installments (IV–V, IX–XIII) are about immigrant letters, beginning with an account of the work of a governmental Emigration Commission that collected many such letters in 1843 and 1844. He had found only two of these letters in the National Archives, he writes, but the commission's report includes a complete list of all the letters with some "rather long excerpts in the commission's letter journal kept in the Ministry of Social Affairs." Malmin was the first scholar to discover that many letters from the early years of emigration were published in newspapers, and many of those he found there were later used by Theodore C. Blegen in his 1955 book *Land of Their Choice: The Immigrants Write Home*. Malmin's concluding installments are topical: church history, Ole Rynning and the Beaver Creek settlement, newspaper notices, Oleanna, and immigrant ballads.

In all the reports and articles he wrote about his work in Norway, Malmin gave special importance to the immigrant letters and urged the importance of collecting them. He made his first pitch for an organized project for the collection of America letters in the eponymous journal of Nordmands-Forbundet before he left Norway, under the heading "Ta vare paa Amerika-brevene" ("Take Care of the America Letters"). Here he gave tidbits from some of the letters he had discovered and insisted that "there were no more valuable sources for a study of our emigration history—indeed for the history of our people in America—than these letters." He expressed his wish that all who had an interest in this history would do what they could to locate them. At this point it was natural for him to point to Nordmands-Forbundet as "the right organization to take the responsibility for such a collection." He repeated his insistence on the importance of the letters in his article in *Familiens Magasin*:

> And then we must not forget to mention the "America letters" as the letters from family and friends in America were called. But they are not to be found in any archive. It was naturally impossible for me to do much with them except to use the newspapers to make people aware of their great historical value and of the need to preserve them. I was given access to some private collections.

Here he also explained why his appeal was an urgent one: "In Norway people often told me that they had had a whole box of old letters from relatives in America, 'but then mother died and none of us was interested in having all these old letters lying around.'" Malmin further concluded his forty-nine-page report to the Carnegie Institution with a statement on the letters:

Some of the most valuable and interesting material on emigration is found scattered about the country in the form of letters from emigrants to their relatives and friends. An organized effort to collect such letters would be a most praiseworthy undertaking. While it has not been possible for the writer to locate much of this material, mention should be made of two private collections.

These two collections are described in the tenth and thirteenth installments in *Decorah-Posten*: One is a collection of copies made by Abraham Grimstvedt and the other a collection of letters Elise Wærenskjold wrote in the period 1852 to 1892 in the possession of Emil Olsen.[22] Malmin brought the copies of letters made by Grimstvedt back to America and deposited them in the Luther College Library, where they were forgotten. When Øyvind Gulliksen discovered them in the college archives in the 1990s no one could explain why they were there. Evidently all did not share Gunnar Malmin's understanding of the value of the immigrant letters.

The young Gunnar Malmin's pioneering work is truly impressive. In the early years of Blegen's editorship at NAHA, Malmin took part in the work of translating, annotating, and editing some of the sources he had uncovered in the course of a few hectic months in Norway or "over there" as he called the country of his ancestors in a note to his introductory article in *Decorah-Posten*.[23] Soon after his return to the United States, however, he concluded that he was more interested in music than in history. After graduate study in music at Northwestern University and the University of Michigan, concluded with a master's degree from the latter institution, he eventually became a professor of music at Pacific Lutheran University in Tacoma, Washington, where he also was choir director for

---

22. Gulliksen published the Grimstvedt letters in 1999 as *"Saa nær hverandre": Ei samling Amerikabrev fra Midtvesten til Nissedal 1850–1875*. A draft translation of these letters is in the NAHA archives. Wærenskjold letters have been published as *The Lady with the Pen: Elise Wærenskjold in Texas*, ed. C. A. Clausen (Northfield, Minn.: Norwegian-American Historical Association, 1961) and in the present edition.

23. Gunnar J. Malmin was translator and editor of "Bishop Jacob Neumann's Word of Admonition to the Peasants" (1926) and "The Disillusionment of an Immigrant: Sjur Jørgensen Haaeim's 'Information on Conditions in North America'" (1928) in the first and third volumes respectively in the NAHA annual journal *Norwegian American Studies and Records*, and of the book *America in the Forties: The Letters of Ole Munch Ræder*, published by NAHA in 1929. He had written about his discovery of both Munch Ræder and Adam Løvenskjold and their reports in his letter to Knut Gjerset of January 15, 1924.

many years.[24] Others were to follow his lead in establishing an organized collection of immigrant letters in Norway.

A NORWEGIAN PARTNER: GUDRUN NATRUD

In November of 1924, Knut Gjerset received a letter from Gudrun Emilie Natrud (1888–1967), an independent scholar in Oslo, offering to assist him in archival research. "It would greatly please me if you at some later date would have use for my assistance. I met Malmin when he was working in the National Archives and he told me that he had found much that he could use."[25] Gunnar Malmin had found that Natrud was both helpful and experienced in archival research; he recommended her to both Gjerset and Theodore Blegen, who wrote to her on May 14, 1925, asking whether it would be possible for her to be of assistance in the collection of immigrant letters. For some time Blegen had been involved in the discussions that eventually led to the founding of the Norwegian-American Historical Association; for him and for others the collection and preservation of immigrant letters was a central task for the planned organization. Blegen's letter to Natrud has not been preserved but her reply dated June 15 makes clear that Blegen had had quite an ambitious project in mind but that he had considerable doubt about the budget that would be available for such a project. Natrud was eager to begin:

> It would make me very happy if the Norwegian-American Historical Society [sic] could make use of my work. I cannot be precise about the cost of the kind of project you have outlined in our correspondence since at this point I do not know how long this work will continue. I have merely skimmed through some of the sources in the National Archives, namely the consular reports and the cabinet discussions you have

24. See Malmin's obituary in the *Tacoma News Tribune*, August 11, 2000, in the Rowberg Scrapbook in the NAHA archives. Malmin wrote to Theodore C. Blegen about his decision to devote himself to music rather than history on September 21, 1927, in his own modest manner: "I guess I'm not much of a musician, I'm no performer and not much of a composer. Just the same, I should still expect to seek a college position teaching History of Music, some theory, and probably directing musical organizations." NAHA, Theodore C. Blegen Papers, P1000, Box 1, File 2

25. NAHA, Knut Gjerset Papers, P683, Box 1, file 2. There is a short biography of Gudrun Emilie Natrud at *arkivportalen.no*, a website that makes it possible to search in all Norwegian archives. She was a very active scholar, familiar with Norwegian archives as well as archives in Stockholm, Copenhagen, and the Vatican. She was employed by *Norsk historisk kjeldeskriftinstitutt*, where Theodore C. Blegen later placed the collection of immigrant letters that is the source for most letters included in this edition. She was awarded His Majesty the King's Gold Medal. There are several references to Natrud's assistance in publications by Blegen and other Norwegian-American scholars.

mentioned concerning the emigration question. Both of these are quite sizable. Nor can I say much about the cost of advertisements, mailings, and office supplies for the projected collecting of America letters. In the event it could be realized, I had planned to correspond with the Norwegian local newspapers (or an informed selection of these) and both place advertisements there and ask the editors to recommend the project in editorials. Moreover, I believe it would be useful to send requests to existing local history societies. If farmers who sent us letters could be reimbursed for any mailing expenses, this would greatly facilitate the collection project... However, it must be assumed that many farmers will want to have their old America letters returned. I would therefore suggest that a sum of money be placed in a bank or with an organization such as Nordmands-Forbundet or perhaps the Government Archives [*Statsarkivet*] for running expenses for advertisements, postage, etc. and that I send you accounts of my expenditures at the end of every month.[26]

She would, of course, require an honorarium for her work. Fredrik Scheel,[27] the head of the Oslo Government Archives, who was also acquainted with Malmin and his work, had advised her to ask for a monthly payment of $60 for three hours a day or a total of 75 hours per month. Scheel had also offered to let the letter project use the Oslo Government Archives as address so that it could more easily gain the confidence of those who had letters in their possession.

Natrud's letter suggests that at this early stage she had a good grasp of possible procedures for an immigrant letter project, but Blegen's correspondence with her had been premature. Blegen had believed that NAHA would be founded at a meeting in St. Paul on July 8 and that he would play a central role in its leadership. Nothing came of this meeting, however. When NAHA eventually was established at a meeting at St. Olaf College in Northfield on October 6, Blegen's role as editor and historian was undisputed, but he had no position on the board where decisions that required funding were made.[28] In Oslo, Natrud waited impatiently for a

---

26. NAHA, Theodore C. Blegen Papers, P1000, Box 1, file 2; my translation. This letter's reference to their correspondence suggests that there had been several letters between them before this one. Natrud wrote in Norwegian, and Blegen responded in English.

27. His full name was Andreas Fredrik Grøn Scheel.

28. Hustvedt, "The Norwegian-American Historical Association and Its Antecedents," 303. Hustvedt suggests that the failed July 8 meeting and another meeting organized by Gjerset and Prestgard on July 24 in Decorah, both opposed by "a group with O. E. Rølvaag at the helm," may be seen as part of a struggle for control of the new association. Rølvaag was a professor at St. Olaf College and as the first secretary of NAHA he had a decisive role in the shaping of the association.

response from Blegen to her June 15 letter and Scheel advised her to write again. In an undated letter to Blegen, she hoped that "the project now has gone beyond the preliminary stage" and reported that Scheel had placed a fireproof room in the Government Archives at their disposal for the safe-keeping of any document they might receive. Scheel had also given her advice on possible procedures for the collection of letters and she concluded specifying some of the archival research she might do while waiting for the submission of letters.[29] Natrud's impatience seems reasonable and in St. Paul Blegen had also been impatient. In the course of the summer of 1925, however, he realized that his initiative had been premature. When he had begun his correspondence with Gudrun Natrud, he seems to have been convinced that the organization of a new historical association, where he saw himself playing a central role, was then only a question of a few simple formalities. Discussions and planning had after all gone on for more than a year and he had drafted the bylaws that he expected would be accepted at the meeting he assumed would be held on July 8 during the centennial celebrations in St. Paul. His letter of May 14 had made both Gudrun Natrud and Andreas F. G. Scheel interested in cooperating with the new association in creating a collection of immigrant letters in Norway. After he had sent his letter to Natrud, however, Blegen was faced with the problematic fact that not only did such an association not yet exist but that it seemed impossible to arrive at an agreement about where it should be placed and how it should be organized. After NAHA was finally organized on October 6, with Blegen at the head of an editorial committee but without any influence on the governing board, it became obvious to him that a project of the format he had first imagined would not be possible. He shared his views with Gudrun Natrud who wrote to him on December 1, 1925, that "in case there is not sufficient funding for the board to begin work on the scale that I have suggested I would be willing to begin working on a more modest scale, for instance two hours a day or two hours every other day or at a set number of hours per month at the payment scale I have mentioned in earlier letters," and she expressed her willingness to search in the archives for anything he may suggest. Blegen wrote to her December 12, most likely in response to her undated letter, thanking her for her "courteous and willing attitude" and saying that he had submitted her letters to the NAHA President, Rev. D. G. Ristad "with the recommendation that the Association adopt the proposal and proceed with the work." On December 23 he wrote again

29. NAHA, Theodore C. Blegen Papers, P1000, Box 1, File 2.

and could now report that Ristad "is thoroughly in sympathy with your plan also for securing the cooperation of people in the various Norwegian localities.[30] That Blegen continued to plan a project for the collection of immigrant letters in Norway is evident in his correspondence with J. Franklin Jameson of the Carnegie Institution in Washington in the spring of 1927, a correspondence primarily concerned with a request to send a copy of Gunnar Malmin's report to the Institution. He thanks him for the report in a letter dated June 2, 1927, where he adds that the NAHA board of editors has "worked out a tentative program for our Norwegian agent (Natrud) and Mr. Prestgard has already started for Norway."[31] The details of this program have not been preserved but it is clear that they relied to a great extent on the contribution of Gudrun Natrud, that she was paid through the involvement of the U.S. ambassador in Norway, L. S. Swenson, and that her work depended largely on the documents discovered by Gunnar Malmin. Blegen evidently found her both reliable and fully qualified and she continued to do archival work for Blegen and NAHA following Blegen's visit to Norway in 1929.[32] She was also involved in the work to establish a project for the collection and preservation of immigrant letters. In a letter she wrote to Prestgard on February 20, 1928, she reports on Professor Oscar Albert Johnsen's endeavors to collect immigrant letters as well as to her own cooperation with Blegen and Malmin. She concludes her report: "This is one of the most fascinating projects I have been involved in! I can only hope that the work to save the old America letters will pick up speed before it is too late."[33]

THE NORWEGIAN-AMERICAN HISTORICAL ASSOCIATION TAKES OVER: KRISTIAN PRESTGARD

For a brief period after the formal establishment of NAHA, Blegen was on the sidelines and the NAHA executive board took on a more active role in

---

30. NAHA, Theodore C. Blegen Papers, P1000, Box 1, File 2. Natrud's letters are written in Norwegian and are quoted in my translation. Blegen wrote to her in English.

31. NAHA, Theodore C. Blegen Papers, P1000, Box 1, File 2.

32. NAHA, Theodore C. Blegen Papers, P1000, Box 1, File 2. The details of her work and the nature of her salary may be seen in correspondence to, from, and about Natrud in the following letters: Blegen to Karl Knudsen, December 17, 1927, Blegen to Natrud, February 22 and June 7, 1928, Natrud to Blegen, June 11 and June 22, 1928, and Blegen to Natrud, June 22, 1928. Natrud continued to work closely with Blegen during his stay in Norway, as demonstrated in a letter she wrote to him on September 18, 1928 (Box 1, File 3).

33. NAHA, Kristian Prestgard Papers, P577, Box 1, File 4.

the work to establish a collection of immigrant letters in Norway. Blegen was very active as editor, however. The first three volumes of *Studies and Records* were published in 1926, 1927, and 1928 and the two first volumes in NAHA's Travel and Description Series, both edited and translated by Blegen, were published in 1926 and 1927. Moreover, he continued his correspondence with Gudrun Natrud, whose role in the creation of a collection of immigrant letters in Norway remained an active one.

The members of the board of the new Association agreed that the collection and preservation of historical sources should be a main task. Kristian Prestgard, the editor of *Decorah-Posten* and one of the new Association's board members, insisted in an editorial published on December 8, 1925, that the collection of immigrant letters should be given priority.[34] But Prestgard, much like Blegen before him, was trying to move too fast. At least this was the view of Ole Edvart Rølvaag, novelist, professor at St. Olaf College, and secretary of the Association. He appears to have asked Prestgard to cease communicating with the other board members in the pages of his newspaper. Prestgard responded in a letter to Rølvaag dated February 8, 1926, where he suggested a division of tasks among the members of the board that he had already discussed with Knut Gjerset, also a member of the board: "Blegen must take the responsibility for our publications. Gjerset will be responsible for the collection of materials and sources here in America. And I will do the same in Norway. That will give all of us a substantial job—of course with the help of all you others. And then I won't write any more about the Association in '*Posten*.' For myself I have *figra ud* [figured out] a complete machinery for our work in Norway, but that is something we can talk about later."[35]

Prestgard's "machinery" did not include government archives and academically trained historians. His December 8, 1925 editorial in *Decorah-Posten* does not mention historians as much as it does useful collaborators. His program is "to establish contacts with organizations in Norway, for instance the rural youth associations, that can get a "letter hunt" going, walking from farm to farm and croft to croft looking for old America

34. Prestgard reprinted much of this editorial in the first of his two books about his visit to Norway in the summer of 1927, *En sommer i Norge 1: Fra den gamle heimbygd* (A Summer in Norway 1: From the Old Home Village), (Minneapolis: Augsburg Publishing House, 1928), 130–132.

35. NAHA, Ole Edvart Rølvaag Papers, P584, Box 6, File 6. This file includes correspondence from June 5, 1915 to December 18, 1926. Prestgard and Rølvaag corresponded in Norwegian. Quotations are in my translation. The Norwegian phrase *figra ud* (figured out) is an instance of the kind of code-switching often used in informal exchanges.

letters—yes, new ones too." When he wrote to Rølvaag on February 8, 1926, about getting "in touch with all the local historians that I know or know of in Norway" about drafting them "into our collection project over there," these were primarily self-taught amateurs in rural Norway, such as his friend Ivar Kleiven whom he called "the Snorre of the Gudbrandsdal Valley."[36] The institutions that had fostered such local historians were the many rural folk high schools, not Norway's single university.

Kristian Prestgard had entered the world of the Scandinavian folk high school culture in the spring of 1885 when he went on foot from his home in Heidal to Vonheim, the school founded and led by Christopher Bruun, in Gausdal.[37] After completing the course offered there he spent some time at Viggo Ullmann's school in Seljord in Telemark before he went on to Denmark in 1886, first staying at a small school near Randers and then attending a two-year course at the folk high school in Askov, a school that attracted students from all the Nordic countries. Returning to Norway in 1888, he taught at the Seljord school, beginning what he hoped would be a lifelong career as a folk high school teacher. But several unfortunate circumstances forced him to look for other possibilities and in 1893 he eagerly accepted an appointment as correspondent for several Norwegian newspapers to the World's Columbian Exhibition in Chicago. This became his introduction to a career in the Norwegian-American press.[38]

When Prestgard set out to organize the work to collect America letters in Norway, it was natural for him to look to people who would have close relations with the folk high school movement for assistance. So he wrote to *Noregs ungdomslag*, a national association of rural youth, at that time led by Olav Midtun, on March 30.[39] The late response dated July 3, 1926, was discouraging. Not only had the board demonstrated their lack of interest in the matter and simply passed the issue on to another association, but Midtun explained that he had concluded his term as chair of the youth association

36. Prestgard, *En sommer i Norge 1*, 116; my translation.

37. Heidal and Gausdal are tributary valleys of the long Gudbrandsdal Valley that runs in a north-south direction through central southeastern Norway.

38. See Kristian Prestgard, "Folkehøiskoler i Norge og Danmark" in *Fra Heidal til Decorah: Veien jeg gikk* (Lesja, Norway: Snøhetta Forlag, 1996), 46–101.

39. Olav Midtun later became a professor at the University of Oslo and was the first director of the Norwegian Broadcasting Corporation (NRK). *Noregs ungdomslag* was closely associated with the movements to further the use of *nynorsk* (New Norwegian), an alternative official version of the Norwegian language created in the mid-nineteenth century and based on rural dialects, mainly from western Norway.

and could no longer be of any assistance in the matter.[40] Prestgard gave vent to his discouragement in a letter to Rølvaag on October 17, 1926:

> Those youth association people there at home in Norway, who I had such great expectations for, are hopeless. After waiting for four months I had a reply of four lines from the chairman telling me that they had passed on the matter to *somebody else*. I thanked him for this information and added that I happened to be from Gudbrandsdal and had no intention of giving up, even if I would have to go back home to Norway and in person walk from farm to farm all over the entire country and collect what we were looking for.

He added that he had written to Professor Oscar Albert Johnsen who was not only interested in the work of their new historical association but was chair of *Landslaget for lokalhistorie* (The National Association for Local History). "I will try," Prestgard wrote, "to get this local history association to make the part of our work that must be done in Norway their concern." And then he added some words that now may seem uncannily prescient: "It has become so awkward to organize this by correspondence. And slow. So it seems that I will have to go home myself and get this done."[41] As if in answer to his frustrated words to Rølvaag, Prestgard received an invitation from the Norwegian Ministry of Foreign Affairs to visit Norway that summer as one of twelve "prominent representatives of the press." The letter, dated April 30, 1927, was from the Norwegian legation in Washington, D.C., and Prestgard immediately wrote back thanking them for the invitation and asking whether it would be possible for him to leave one month before the official tour, on June 7 instead of July 7. There were no objections to his request and a letter dated May 13 confirmed that a berth on the passenger ship *Bergensfjord* had been reserved.[42]

The Norway that Kristian Prestgard felt at home in was rather different from the one that Theodore C. Blegen, who worked for the Minnesota Historical Society and the University of Minnesota, found it natural to approach: few if any of the local historians Prestgard had in mind were academically trained. In his memoirs, Prestgard writes that the folk high schools were not about "educating scholars or specialists or even professionals. The universities do this. The special project of the folk high school was the creation of an educated rural youth who would return to the

---

40. NAHA, Kristian Prestgard Papers, P577, Box 1, File 3.

41. NAHA, Ole Edvart Rølvaag Papers, P584, Box 6, File 6; my translation.

42. NAHA, Kristian Prestgard Papers, P577, Box 1, File 3

farm and continue to cultivate the soil and never become professionals or public servants. For these young people exams for a degree were pedantry and cramming."[43] But for Blegen, a Ph.D. and historian who was to become professor and dean at the University of Minnesota, a degree was a testimony of professionalism and learning. Consequently, he and Prestgard had rather different approaches to the collection of immigrant letters in Norway. But Prestgard was not entirely a stranger to academia and one of his initiatives turned out to be crucial for the project.

One of the people he approached during his visit to Norway in 1927 was Professor Oscar Albert Johnsen, founder and chair of the Norwegian Local History Association. On meeting him, Prestgard realized that Johnsen was already well acquainted with his project and also with his failed attempt to interest *Noregs ungdomslag* in his cause. Indeed, Johnsen had reprinted Prestgard's article on America letters (first published in *Decorah-Posten* on December 8, 1925) in the journal of the Local History Association, *Heimen*. As editor, Johnsen had added his recommendation of the project to collect immigrant letters in Norway and also praised the work done by Gunnar J. Malmin.[44] His meeting with Professor Johnsen must have been like a homecoming for Prestgard. He also met with two other prominent professors of history, Halvdan Koht and Jacob Worm-Müller, with whom he had corresponded before going to Norway. Prestgard's closest relations, however, were not with these academic historians but with the self-taught local historian Ivar Kleiven, a friend of his youth.

Kristian Prestgard played an important role in the early work to initiate the collection of immigrant letters that eventually found a home in the Norwegian National Archives. In his book about his visit to Norway, *En sommer i Norge*, he was overly optimistic when he wrote: "When I left Norway it seemed agreed that the Association for Local History was to organize a systematic collection of old America letters for our Historical Association at their own expense."[45] Even though Professor Johnsen remained a supporter of the immigrant letter project, Prestgard's most

---

43. Prestgard, "Folkehøiskoler i Norge og Danmark," 46–47; my translation.

44. Oscar Albert Johnsen, "Amerikabrevene: Oprop fra Det norsk-amerikanske historielag" (The America Letters: A Call from the Norwegian-American Historical Association) in *Heimen: Tidsskrift ugitt av Landslaget for Bygde- og Byhistorie 2* (1926), 43–45.

45. Prestgard, *En sommer i Norge*, 132–133; my translation. Prestgard writes about his visit with Ivar Kleiven in the chapter titled "Ivar Kleiven: Gudbrandsdalens Snorre," 116–128. The two had been friends since their early youth. See Halvard Grude Forfang, *Ivar Kleiven 1854–1934* (Oslo: Aschehoug, 1945).

important contribution to this project may have been his good relations with Sir Karl Knudsen, a Norwegian who had become a highly successful English businessman in London.

A PATRON STEPS ONTO THE SCENE: SIR KARL KNUDSEN

The Chicago businessman Birger Osland was the first treasurer of the Norwegian-American Historical Association, an office he held until 1951.[46] His contribution to the first quarter century of the Association was crucial for its success. For the early years of NAHA, particularly the efforts to create a collection of immigrant letters in Norway, it turned out that Osland's introduction of his friend Karl Knudsen to the Association was of particular importance. Osland and Knudsen had become close friends after a visit the latter made to Chicago in 1921. When Osland learned that Knudsen would be traveling in the United States in 1926, he suggested that his friend make Decorah, Iowa, a part of his itinerary so that he could sit in on the NAHA board meeting there on May 26.[47] Prestgard, a member of the board, wrote to Rølvaag, the NAHA secretary, on October 17 about "the blessed Sir Karl. Surely it was by design of Providence that he should happen to be here just at the time we had our meeting."[48] He also wrote about Knudsen's presence at this board meeting in his narrative of his summer in Norway:

> And Sir Karl sat faithfully with us the entire day. He was so engaged in our cause that he every now and then gave us good advice on difficult or sensitive issues. He was particularly interested in the report on how the young Gunnar Malmin had come back from Norway a couple of years earlier with a valuable treasure of Norwegian-American historical source material. He also noted that NAHA wanted to continue his work and establish a branch of its research endeavors in Norway.[49]

Knudsen seems to have enjoyed himself at this board meeting and he was impressed by what he learned there about the achievements of NAHA in its first couple of years. He wrote to the NAHA president D. G. Ristad from London on April 22, 1927, that "my short visit out there with you has made a deep impression and strengthened my awareness of the abilities and

46. See his memoirs: Birger Osland, *A Long Pull from Stavanger: The Reminiscences of a Norwegian Immigrant* (Northfield, Minn.: Norwegian-American Historical Association, 1940).

47. Correspondence between Karl Knudsen and Birger Osland is in the Birger Osland Papers, NAHA.

48. NAHA, Ole Edvart Rølvaag Papers, P584, Box 6, File 6; my translation.

49. Prestgard, *En sommer i Norge*, 135; my translation.

mission of our race. I hope to return next year, preferably at the time when the wheat is ready for harvesting. Would it then be too impossibly hot?"[50]

Karl Knudsen was a man of action. However, one of his attempts to establish such "a branch of [NAHA's] research endeavors in Norway" turned out to be of limited value. During a visit to Oslo later that year he met Simon Christian Hammer, a journalist and historian who was known to both Knudsen and the NAHA board members from his brief stint as Secretary General and editor of Nordmands-Forbundet.[51] When Knudsen invited Hammer to do research work for NAHA, he seems to have been unaware of Blegen's relationship with Gudrun Natrud through the recommendation of Gunnar Malmin. Hammer welcomed an opportunity for some extra income. When Knudsen wrote to D. G. Ristad, the president of NAHA, from London on April 22, 1927, however, he seems to have been in doubt about the limitations of the man he had appointed: "I do not exactly have the impression that Hammer will be the best man for us."[52] According to the arrangement he had with Knudsen, Hammer was to work for NAHA for 100 *kroner* a month and begin as soon as he received an authorization from Rølvaag. Rølvaag wrote to him, referring to a letter he had had from Knudsen from London, dated November 8, about the work he should do: typing copies of relevant newspaper articles, collecting pamphlets and similar publications on emigration, and collecting immigrant letters. He added that Prestgard had been in touch with Professor Oscar Albert Johnsen about the collection of letters and that Hammer should not do anything that might interfere with this project.[53] Hammer did some work for NAHA but it appears that the results of his efforts were of little value. At least this is Theodore Blegen's evaluation in a letter he wrote to Gudrun Natrud on June 22, 1928.[54]

---

50. NAHA, Ditlef G. Ristad Papers, P582, Box 2, File 1.

51. Odd S. Lovoll, *Celebrating a Century: Nordmands-Forbundet and Norwegians in the World Community 1907–2007* (Oslo: Nordmands-Forbundet, 2009), 52. S. C. Hammer was Secretary General of Nordmands-Forbundet and editor of its eponymous journal from late 1917 to his resignation in early 1919. This was a period when "a stagnant, or even declining, membership, and a budget deficit gave cause for concern."

52. NAHA, Ditlef G. Ristad Papers, P582, Box 2, File 1; my translation.

53. NAHA, Ole Edvart Rølvaag Papers, P584, Box 6, File 8. The copy of this letter is undated.

54. NAHA, Theodore C. Blegen Papers P1000, Box 1, File 2. "Hr. Hammer did nothing of the slightest consequence for the Association during the time when he was in its employ. The materials turned over to us by Hr. Hammer are now in my possession but they are not worth sending on to you… I regret to say that he must have treated the appointment as a sinecure."

Karl Knudsen's main contribution to the immigrant letter project in Norway was his financial support and his good relationship with the American ambassador to Norway, the Norwegian-American Laurits S. Swenson. Prestgard was overjoyed when he wrote to Rølvaag from Norway, on August 18, 1927, about the generosity of Knudsen: "He has opened an account for us here in an Oslo bank with five thousand *kroner*. – May God bless him."[55] The pamphlet "A Review and a Challenge" published by NAHA in 1938 pays special tribute to Knudsen:

> In Norway, thanks to a fund created by the late Karl Knudsen, the Association in 1928 began a successful campaign to obtain old "America books"; transcripts of "America letters," which are invaluable as source materials; photostats of newspaper items and copies of official and unofficial documents; film photographs of "America letters," archival material, and newspaper articles, secured in co-operation with the Library of Congress; a calendar of Norwegian archival materials dealing with American history and emigration, prepared by Mrs. Gudrun Natrud of Oslo; transcripts of Munch Raeder letters from originals in Norway, and Photostats of certain significant pamphlets, books, book titles, and documents. Many of these materials were collected by Dr. Blegen and utilized by him in the writing of his *Norwegian Migration to America*.
>
> The original fund created in Norway by Sir Karl for the collection of materials bearing on emigration was augmented by a later gift from the same generous friend of the Association. He was a native of Norway who later became a British subject. His dormant interest in the Norwegian-American element was stirred into activity when he read Rølvaag's *Giants in the Earth*. This interest took tangible form during a visit to the Northwest. He became a life member of the Norwegian-American Historical Association and, as we have seen, made financial provisions for historical research in Norway. His death last November took from the membership role an ardent supporter of the Association.[56]

55. NAHA, Ole Edvart Rølvaag Papers, P584, Box 6, File 7; my translation. Indeed, Rølvaag was sure that Karl Knudsen had provided the funding for the official visit of the group of American newspaper editors the summer of 1927. "He did exactly the same thing for some English and Scottish "newspapermen" and paid every cent from his own pocket." Letter to Prestgard, April 27, 1927. He repeats this in another letter to Prestgard on May 11, 1927. NAHA, Ole Edvart Rølvaag Papers, P584, Box 6, File 7.

56. NAHA, "A Review and a Challenge" (Northfield, Minn.: Norwegian-American Historical Association, 1938), 11. A review of NAHA's endowment funds on page 22 concludes: "It may be added that the grand total as given above does not include the generous fund set up by Sir Karl Knudsen for the promotion of research and the collecting of records in Norway."

By the time Knudsen had made these arrangements, Blegen had taken responsibility for the further work to collect America letters in Norway and he had appointed Gudrun Natrud as his assistant.[57] Blegen was now ready to go to Norway himself.

AN AMERICAN HISTORIAN TAKES COMMAND:
THEODORE C. BLEGEN

When Prestgard was invited by the Norwegian Ministry of Foreign Affairs to visit Norway in the summer of 1927 as a member of a group of American newspaper editors, he had been visible to his Norwegian hosts because of his recognized status in his ethnic group as editor of one of the largest Norwegian immigrant newspapers in the United States. When Blegen traveled to Norway as one of the American representatives at the International Congress of Historians held in Oslo in August 1928, he had been selected to represent the prestigious American Historical Association because of his scholarly qualifications, not because of his ethnicity.[58] Blegen's invitation to present a paper on Norwegian immigration to his international colleagues at the congress was a confirmation of the early success of his ambition to address an audience beyond the narrow confines of his ethnic group. The founders of NAHA had been divided on the question of the language of their publications: Norwegian or English. Blegen had never been in doubt. As he wrote to Knut Gjerset on September 30, 1926, about the first NAHA publication, a bilingual edition of Ole Rynning's *True Account of America* (1838), "a Norwegian text with a Norwegian introduction will make the work of very little value a generation hence." He concluded his six-point

---

57. NAHA, Theodore C. Blegen Papers, P1000, Box 1, File 2. Blegen too was in contact with Knudsen and kept him informed about "the editorial and publication activities" of NAHA. "I feel that cooperation is vital to the success of the attempt to gather and preserve the letters and diaries of immigrants that may yet be extant in Norway, and in this connection I must say that I was very much pleased to hear from Mr. Prestgard about your own endeavors to promote the work last summer."

58. Prestgard had little experience of academia. His world was that of his immigrant group. When he heard of Blegen's invitation he thought it was unfair that Knut Gjerset had not been given the same honor and wrote to Professor Halvdan Koht in Oslo inquiring why they had not invited Gjerset. Koht replied on March 23, 1928, that Blegen had been nominated by the American Historical Association. "So you will understand that we cannot on our own approach Knut Gjerset. I would be very happy to have Gjerset at the Congress and I have asked our secretary to send him the available information; but it is normally the American committee … that takes care of the distribution of this material over there." NAHA, Kristian Prestgard Papers, P577, Box 1, File 3; my translation.

argument for the use of English with a statement that may stand as his program for his work as an American historian:

> I am convinced that the time has come for us Norwegian-Americans to move out upon a larger stage—to bring out our records in the most definitive form with a view not only to our own people (including the older and the younger generations) but also to the American people in general. Indeed I may say that one of the big reasons why I went into this association was that I felt that the time was ripe for putting our historical records before the people of the whole country. I am much interested in the preservation as long as possible of the Norwegian language among Norwegian-Americans, but I feel that we will lose more than we will gain if we use our publications to forward the Norwegian language movement.[59]

By 1928, in spite of his many and demanding tasks, Blegen had already placed himself at the forefront of American immigration historians. But he had not yet had time to focus on what he regarded as his main project, a history of the Norwegian immigration to the United States. He was the Assistant Superintendent of the Minnesota Historical Society and, as he wrote to Gjerset on December 15, 1926, he had many other responsibilities:

> I teach six hours a week at Hamline [University in St. Paul] and I am head of the history department; ... I am editing the quarterly magazine of this society, acting as executive secretary for the endowment campaign in Minnesota of the American Historical Association; serving as managing editor for the N.A.H.A.; and in-between times I have prepared an article and a batch of documents for the yearbook of the Swedish Historical Society of America, which is just being published, the latter being a contribution of about one hundred pages. That I can do all these things, however, is possible only because my health is good and I have excellent assistance.[60]

The invitation to present a paper at the International Congress of Historians in Oslo opened many doors for Blegen. This was the best possible introduction to historians in Norway and it strengthened his application for a scholarship for a year in Norway with his family.

Ole Edvart Rølvaag, novelist and professor at St. Olaf College, may well have been the NAHA board member who had the greatest awareness of the inestimable value of Blegen's contribution to the fledgling association. In

59. NAHA, Knut Gjerset Papers, P683, Box 1, File 2.

60. NAHA, Knut Gjerset Papers, P 683, Box 1, File 2.

January 1927 Rølvaag raised the question of an annual stipend for Blegen from NAHA with the treasurer Birger Osland: "All in all, I don't know what we could have done without him." Osland, however, who played a key role in the development of NAHA in its first decades, realized that the new association could not possibly manage to pay a salary to its editor. But when Blegen wrote to Osland on July 15, 1928, asking whether NAHA would be able to cover his travel expenses for participation in the Congress in Oslo, Osland immediately responded that "a limited amount should be provided." This "limited amount" was later set at $250.[61] Blegen had decided to stay in Norway for an extended period by the time he wrote to Karl Knudsen on December 17, 1927. Soon after this he also began communication with Prestgard about his work to involve the National Association for Local History in the letter project.[62] In Oslo, Gudrun Natrud had received a contract from NAHA and, with the assistance and generosity of Karl Knudsen, she was able to receive her salary as well as money for her expenses from the American ambassador to Norway, the Norwegian American Laurits S. Swenson. She wrote to Prestgard on February 20, 1928, that only a few letters had been received by the National Association, "only forty to fifty letters, they say, and among them a collection of thirty-two letters from Mrs. Hansteen." But Professor Johnsen had explained that "their method of collecting the letters through the local associations will work slowly, so we may not see the results until late summer, after they have been able to use the winter for their meetings."[63]

Prestgard evidently realized that he had now done what he could for the letter project and that it was time for a professional historian to step in and have the main responsibility for its further development.[64] Blegen's letter to Gudrun Natrud on February 22, 1928, written without knowledge

61. NAHA, Birger Osland Papers, P574, Box 16, File 4.

62. NAHA, Theodore C. Blegen Papers, P1000, Box 1, File 2.

63. NAHA, Kristian Prestgard Papers, P577, Box 1, File 4; my translation.

64. Prestgard's contribution was recognized by all and he was by no means pushed aside. In the Chicago magazine *Norden* (December 1930), Sigrid T. Hakstad writes about Blegen's work in Norway and reports that a two-volume edition of letters was planned with Prestgard as editor. Prestgard, however, was modest about his qualifications and recognized that the younger generation of academic historians in the Association represented a level of professionalism that he was not educated for. He wrote to Rølvaag on December 22, 1929, that he wished to retire from NAHA's editorial board and leave the work there to the historians Blegen, Gjerset, and Laurence M. Larson: "This should be a professional board and four members should be sufficient. But they must all be historians, and I do not belong in that company. I have nominated the young Malmin for my place on the Board." NAHA, Ole Edvart Rølvaag Papers, P584, Box 6, File 7; my translation.

of the report she had submitted to Prestgard two days earlier, was his first communication with her since his premature correspondence in 1925. It is evident that he appreciated the work she had already completed: "I shall want to depend to a very considerable extent upon your advice," he wrote. Some of what she had accomplished may be seen in the report she sent to Blegen June 11.[65] When Blegen arrived in Norway later that summer with a stipend from the Guggenheim Foundation, the ground was well laid and he had full confidence in the assistant who was waiting for him.

While the first two NAHA emissaries, Malmin and Prestgard, had been rather anonymous figures on their expeditions to Norway, Blegen's movements and achievements during his visit to Norway may be followed in notices and interviews in Norwegian as well as in Norwegian-American newspapers. Indeed, from the collection of clippings in the Theodore C. Blegen Papers in the NAHA archives it seems that he was interviewed by journalists wherever he went in Norway, and a common refrain in articles they wrote was Blegen's appeal to send any immigrant letters people may possess to Professor Oluf Kolsrud at the Norwegian National Archives.[66]

A HOME FOR THE AMERICA LETTERS: OLUF KOLSRUD

An independent research institute for the collection, preservation, and publication of documents relating to Norwegian history, *Norsk Historisk Kjeldeskrift-Institutt (Historiografisk Samling)*, had been established at the National Archives in Oslo in 1922.[67] From the beginning Professor Oluf Kolsrud was chair of the institute, and as early as 1926, when Professor Oscar Albert Johnsen published his announcement in *Heimen*, Kolsrud's institute was given the institutional responsibility for the collection and preservation of America letters; people who wished to donate such letters were asked to send them there.[68] It was natural that Blegen should regard Kolsrud as his partner and collaborator in Norway. After Blegen had presented his paper on the importance of immigrant letters for immigration history at the international congress, Kolsrud presented an edited version of the paper at a meeting of the Norwegian Academy of Science and Letters (*Det Norske Videnskaps-Akademi*) and had it published in the Academy's

---

65. NAHA, Theodore C. Blegen Papers, P1000, Box 1, File 3.

66. See NAHA, Theodore C. Blegen Papers, P1000, Box 1, File 2.

67. This institute is now a fully integrated department of the National Archives as *Kjeldeskrift-avdelingen*.

68. Oscar Albert Johnsen, "Amerikabrevene," *Heimen* 2 (1926), 45.

series for the humanities.[69] Blegen's paper and his research in Norway received attention far beyond academia. The Oslo newspaper *Tidens Tegn* published a report on Blegen's paper at the congress on August 17, and other newspapers also wrote about Blegen's research and his tour of many areas of Norway.[70] He was interviewed in *Bergens Tidende* on June 2, 1929, the day he left Norway to return to the United States with his family. Here he told about the valuable source material he had discovered, in particular the many America letters: "The work to collect America letters will continue and the permanent archive for these documents will be *Historiografisk samling* (the Institute for Historical Documents at the National Archives) in Oslo. All who are interested in having their America letters preserved should send them there, to Professor Kolsrud. This collection will be of the greatest value at some time in the future."[71] Blegen had often spoken to journalists about his project, making this appeal, since he had come to the country in August 1928. In the pamphlet Kolsrud had published by the Norwegian Academy of Science and Letters, Blegen gave an account of the collaboration between the Norwegian-American Historical Association and the Local History Association in Norway and outlined his vision of an international project:

> Such historical cooperation, if extended, might lead to the discovery and preservation, in many European countries, of new materials of value for an understanding of that vast modern migration which furnishes in its myriad ramifications one of the great themes of American history and which reminds one again of the racial and cultural bonds between the new world and the old.

And he concluded with "a special message to Norwegian readers" on the importance of both the America letters and the letters sent to America from Norway ("Norway letters") for the history that the United States and Norway had in common: "I appeal to those who are interested in this work

---

69 Theodore C. Blegen, *The "America Letters."* Avhandlinger utgitt av Det Norske Videns-kaps-Akademi i Oslo. II. Hist.-Filos. Klasse. 1928. No. 5.

70. An abbreviated version of one of the lectures Blegen gave in Norway is published in *Nordmands-Forbundet* 21 (1928), 295–298.

71. My translation. Other instances of the attention given to Blegen in Norwegian newspapers are in the NAHA archives: NAHA Papers Box 41. The clipping from *Bergens Tidende* has no date. Rølvaag wrote on September 7, 1929, to Birger Osland about a meeting he had with Blegen in St. Paul after his return: "He is effusive in his enthusiasm about his stay in Norway and all that he has found there." NAHA, Birger Osland Papers, P574, Box 18, File 7; my translation.

to come to its active support." They could contact either the Local History Association or Professor Oluf Kolsrud at the National Archives in Oslo:

> Almost every community in Norway has played its part in the emigration movement. It would be too bad if any community were not represented in this national collection of records. Norwegians and Americans have here an opportunity not only to make genuine contributions to their own local and national history, but to inaugurate a kind of historical cooperation that will be watched with interest by the world of historical scholarship.[72]

Publications of the Norwegian Academy of Science and Letters did not usually directly address the population at large and invite them to participate in a scholarly project. For Blegen, however, who worked in and for the Norwegian-American Historical Association, cooperation between professional historians and an actively engaged populace had been essential for the many achievements of the young association.[73] This had been natural both because the professional historians were part of and at home in an immigrant culture, and because the history that was researched and written about was the history of common men and women.

Such a sense of a shared interest was not yet familiar in Norway. Most historians could not imagine a history of Norway that focused on common men and women and in which emigration was seen as a central theme. In a later generation the historian Ingrid Semmingsen would be recognized as a pioneer in making emigration her main area of research, but at the time of Blegen's visit, Oluf Kolsrud was one of only a very few academics

---

72. Blegen, *The "America Letters,"* 24–25. "Norway letters" was Blegen's term for letters sent from Norway to immigrants in the United States. Norwegian historians have only recently begun to understand what a valuable source such letters may be for Norwegian history, in particular local history. A modest program to collect such letters was initiated by the *Norsk lokalhistorisk institutt* (The Norwegian Institute for Local History) in Oslo in 1993.

73. This cooperation was not always unproblematic. Birger Osland, the first NAHA treasurer, was also a major financial contributor and a donation from him made it possible to publish the first volume of Blegen's *Norwegian Migration to America*. Osland, a Chicago businessman, did not want to have any money spent on another Blegen project, a volume of immigrant ballads in English translation, because he found them to be of no literary value. He explained this in a letter to Rølvaag on August 29, 1929: "As a Norwegian-born layman I must be permitted to say that I cannot share the enthusiasm demonstrated by American scholars for such quaint songs." NAHA, Ole Edvart Rølvaag Papers, P584, Box 6, File 5. Gunnar J. Malmin had also seen the value of such ballads and devoted one of the installments of his long account of his findings in Norway to such songs, calling them "America poems" or "Amerika-digte" (*Decorah-Posten*, March 27, 1925). In 1936, Blegen and Martin B. Ruud translated and edited a volume of "quaint songs," titled *Norwegian Emigrant Songs and Ballads*, and published by the University of Minnesota Press, not NAHA. The melodies were harmonized by Gunnar J. Malmin, who here was able to combine his interests in music and immigration history.

who recognized the importance of his project. On August 29, 1929, some weeks after Blegen had returned from Norway, there was a board meeting of *Kjeldeskriftfondet* (the foundation for historical sources). These were prominent Norwegian historians with a special responsibility for the finances and publications of *Norsk Historisk Kjeldeskrift-institutt* (*Historiografisk Samling*), the full name of the institute for the collection and publication of documents relating to Norwegian history at the National Archives. Kolsrud, as chair of the institute, was secretary of the board and presented a brief report on the work that had been done to collect letters, including the agreement to cooperate with the United States Library of Congress. A representative of the Library of Congress had helped to make copies of the letters possible so that the originals could be returned to the owners. He had, according to the minutes of this board meeting, presented Kolsrud with

> an estimate of the cost of copying all the letters that had been given on loan (a total of 396 pages). Kolsrud asked whether *Kjeldeskriftfondet* could contribute the necessary sum to make paper copies of the letters (about 0.60 to 0.65 *kroner* per page), since *Historiografisk Samling* only had the money necessary for copies on film (at 0.07 *kroner* per page). The board expressed its interest in the collection of America letters, but could not accept any expenditure for the copying of letters in private ownership.[74]

The handwritten minutes were taken by Kolsrud himself and the item concerning the America letters covers more than one page while the other four items discussed by the board at this meeting together cover less than one page. It is evident that we today have such a large collection of immigrant letters in the Norwegian National Archives thanks to the personal interest and initiative of Oluf Kolsrud. There is good reason to be grateful that Kolsrud and Blegen met in August 1928 and that they both saw the immense value of the many letters in chests, drawers, barns, and attics in Norwegian homes. Some years after his return to the United States, Blegen wrote to Kolsrud asking about "additional letters": "It is my impression, from reports I have read, that considerable progress has been made in the work of collecting such materials." He concludes on a more personal note, "with pleasant recollections of my contacts with you and with hearty appreciation of all that you did for me."[75]

74. The minutes of the meetings of *Kjeldeskriftfondet* are in the National Archives; my translation. Evidently, the board members were not impressed by the involvement of the Library of Congress, given their unwillingness to support the project.

75. December 10, 1932; NAHA, Theodore C. Blegen Papers, P1000, Box 1, File 4.

Immigrant letters were an important source for Blegen when he wrote his groundbreaking two volumes of immigration history, *The Norwegian Migration to America* (1931 and 1940). He also edited several volumes of such letters in English translation. One of these volumes is *Frontier Mother: The Letters of Gro Svendsen* (1950), a collection of letters of a young immigrant woman from Hallingdal, a valley to the west of Oslo.[76] While he was at work on *Frontier Mother*, Blegen also published a volume of essays he called *Grass Roots History* (1947), a title that aptly captures the life work of this eminent historian. In one of the essays, "Literature of the Unlettered," he reflects on the value of the letters of Gro Svendsen and many other immigrants both as important sources for historians and as texts that—with some editorial assistance—could give lay readers direct access to lives lived in earlier times. Two concluding paragraphs of this essay reflect on the kind of texts that he was among the first to recognize as pages of a literature that deserve our attention:

> Simple things, yes. But I wonder if these are not some of the basic elements in America's story. The books have much to say about the forces inherent in economics and politics. As one reads this sheaf of letters one quickly realizes that the most striking and notable thing about them is the hunger for education they reveal, a hunger centered by Gro upon her children. To her this was more than a cultural need; she saw it as the pathway to the larger opportunities offered by the New World...
>
> Gro was not unusual in education or in experience. If she was in any respect untypical, it was by virtue of the grace and vividness and precision with which she put her thoughts and experiences down in black and white. If her writing is literature, it is part of the folk literature of America, the literature of the unlettered. Her letters are only one small segment of the masses of letters that I have collected in the valleys to which they were sent.

The collection of immigrant letters in what is now known as *Kjeldeskriftavdelingen* (the Department of Historical Documents) in the Norwegian National Archives is a unique body of texts by women and men that covers a wide span of ages and walks of life. The selection of letters

---

76. Pauline Farseth and Theodore C. Blegen, *Frontier Mother: The Letters of Gro Svendsen* (Northfield, Minn.: Norwegian-American Historical Association, 1950). The first letter by Gro Svendsen's niece and daughter-in-law, Sigri Nilsen, who immigrated in 1891 with her uncle Ole Nilsen, appears in Volume 2 of this edition (2:268). She soon became Sigrid Svendsen after her marriage to the youngest son of her aunt Gro and her later letters are published in Volume 3.

translated for this edition makes this literature of the unlettered available to American readers.

There have been many actors in this narrative of the making of the collection of American immigrant letters in the Norwegian National Archives. From the Norwegian (and British) side it has been natural to call attention to Gudrun Natrud, the amanuensis; Karl Knudsen, the patron; and Oluf Kolsrud, the archivist. Three Americans who in their different ways made contributions that were essential for the creation of the collection are Gunnar J. Malmin, the young pathfinder; Kristian Prestgard, the ardent enthusiast; and Theodore C. Blegen, the organizer, scholar, and author. All historians of the migration from Norway to the United States owe these six a debt of gratitude.

BIBLIOGRAPHY

Immigrant Letters that Appear in Norwegian-American Historical Association Publications

Letters Published in Books

Blegen, Theodore C., ed. 1947. *Frontier Parsonage: The Letters of Olaus Fredrik Duus, Norwegian Pastor in Wisconsin, 1855–1858.* Translated by the Verdandi Study Club of Minneapolis. Northfield, Minn.: Norwegian-American Historical Association.

—. 1955. *Land of Their Choice: The Immigrants Write Home.* Minneapolis: University of Minnesota Press.

Clausen, C. A., ed. 1961. *The Lady with the Pen: Elise Wærenskjold in Texas.* Northfield, Minn.: Norwegian-American Historical Association.

Farseth, Pauline, and Theodore C. Blegen, eds. 1950. *Frontier Mother: The Letters of Gro Svendsen.* Northfield, Minn.: Norwegian-American Historical Association.

Letters Published in *Norwegian-American Studies*

The following list only includes letters sent from the United States to Norway. It is organized chronologically by issue number of *Norwegian-American Studies*. Entries within each issue are ordered alphabetically by author/editor. Where an entry includes several letters, it is ordered according to the date of the first letter. "Nor. ed." following an entry indicates publication in the Norwegian edition of these volumes, *Fra Amerika til Norge*. *Norwegian American Studies* (NAS) was originally published under the name *Norwegian American Studies and Records* for issues 1 through 20.

NAS 3 (1928)

Hovde, Brynjolf J., trans. "Chicago as Viewed by a Norwegian Immigrant in 1864," 65–72.

> From: Christian H. Jevne, *Chicago, Illinois, 10 December 1864*
> To: His parents, *Hamar, Hedmark*

Larson, Henrietta, trans. "An Immigration Journey to America in 1854," 58–64.

> From: Ole Olson Østerud, *Muskego, Racine County, Wisconsin, 21 June 1854*
> To: His brother, *Hurdal, Akershus*

—. "On Lake Erie: An Immigrant Journey from Quebec to Wisconsin in 1852," 92–98.

> *This letter also appears in Blegen*, Land of Their Choice, 1955.
> From: Erik Thorstad, *Ixonia, Jefferson County, Wisconsin, 9 November 1852*
> To: His family, *Øyer, Oppland*

NAS 4 (1929)

Hovde, Brynjolf J., trans. "Three Civil War Letters from 1862," 74–91.

> From: A Soldier, *Camp Butler, Newport News, Virginia, 31 March* and *5 April 1862*, and *Camp Fair Oak, Richmond, Virginia, 19 June 1862*
> To: Unknown

NAS 5 (1930)

Blegen, Theodore C., ed. and trans. "Immigrant Women and the American Frontier: Three Early 'America Letters,'" 14–29.

> From: Janniche Sæhle, *Koshkonong, Dane County, Wisconsin, 28 September 1847*
> To: Johannes Sæhle, *Oslo*

> From: Henrietta Jessen, *Milwaukee, Wisconsin, 20 February 1850*
> To: Eleonore Williamsen, *Hetland, Stavanger, Rogaland*

> From: Guri Olsdatter Rosseland (Endreson), *Harrison, Kandiyohi County, Minnesota, 2 December 1866*
> To: Her family, *Kvam, Hordaland*
> (Nor. ed. II:141)

NAS 7 (1933)

Clausen, C. A., trans. "The Fraser River Gold Rush: An Immigrant Letter of 1858," 47–52.

> From: An unknown immigrant, *Whatcom, Whatcom County, Washington, 12 July 1858*
> To: Someone in Stavanger, Rogaland

Hodnefield, Jacob, trans. "Immigration as Viewed by a Norwegian-American Farmer in 1869," 53–61.

> From: Ole Spillum, *North Cape, Wisconsin, 8 January 1869*
> To: Jørgen Havig, *Overhalla, Nord-Trøndelag*

Unstad, Lyder L., trans. "The First Norwegian Migration into Texas: Four 'America Letters,'" 39–57.

> From: T. Grimseth, *Four Mile Prairie, Van Zandt County, Texas, 20 July 1852*
> To: Taale Andreas Gjestvang, *Løten, Hedmark*

> From: Johan Brunstad, *Four Mile Prairie, Van Zandt County, Texas, 21 July 1852*
> To: Taale Andreas Gjestvang, *Løten, Hedmark*

From: Elise Wærenskjold, *Four Mile Prairie, Van Zandt County, Texas,*
25 July 1852
To: Taale Andreas Gjestvang, *Løten, Hedmark*

From: J. R. Reiersen, *Four Mile Prairie, Van Zandt County, Texas, 27 July 1852*
To: Taale Andreas Gjestvang, *Løten, Hedmark*

NAS 8 (1934)

Johansen, Arne Odd, trans. "Johannes Nordboe and Norwegian Immigration: An 'America Letter' of 1837," 23–38.

From: Johannes Nordboe, *Ottawa, La Salle County, Illinois, 30 April 1837*
To: Hans Larsen Rudi, *Ringebu, Oppland*

NAS 14 (1944)

Bjork, Kenneth, ed. and trans. "Pioneering on the Technical Front: A Story Told in America Letters," 227–234.

From: Hans Peter Herman Krag Hougen, *Philadelphia, Pennsylvania,*
1883-1884
To: Family, *Kragerø, Telemark*

Blegen, Theodore C., ed. and trans. "An Immigrant Exploration of the Middle West in 1839: A Letter by Johannes Johansen and Søren Bache," translated by the Verdandi Study Club of Minneapolis, 41–53.

From: Johannes Johansen and Søren Bache, *Fox River, La Salle County,*
Illinois, 31 December 1830
To: Relatives and friends, *Drammen, Buskerud*

Blegen, Theodore C., ed. and trans. "Behind the Scenes of Emigration: A Series of Letters from the 1840s," 78–116.

From: J. R. Reiersen, *Iowa City, Iowa, 24 January 1844* and *Cincinnati, Ohio,*
10 March 1844
To: Friends, *Kristiansand, Vest-Agder*

These two and other letters were written in Norway.

NAS 15 (1949)

Clausen, C. A., trans. "An Immigrant's Advice on America: Some Letters of Søren Bache," 77–84.

From: Søren Bache, *while on a visit to Norway in 1842–43*
To: C. L. Clausen, E. Bache, Paul Knutzen, and Ole Bjerkrem

NAS 20 (1959)

Clausen, C. A., trans. "A Texan Manifesto: A Letter from Mrs. Elise Wærenskjold" 32–45.

From: Elise Wærenskjold, *Four Mile Prairie, Van Zandt County, Texas,*
9 July 1851
To: Taale Andreas Gjestvang, *Løten, Hedmark*

NAS 21 (1962)

Folkedahl, Beulah, trans. "Norwegians Become Americans," 95–135.

> From: Sjur and Nils Eidsvaag, *Cambridge, Dane County, Wisconsin, 23 September 1849* and *Madison, Dane County, Wisconsin, 12 December 1849*
> To: Family, *Lindaas, Hordaland*

> From: Ole Pedersen, *Columbus, Wisconsin, 22 October 1855*
> To: Hans Lindaas, *Lindaas, Hordaland*

> From: Endre and Matthianne Eidsvaag, *Deerfield, Wisconsin, 7 February 1856*
> To: Hans and Karl Lindaas, *Lindaas, Hordaland*

> *Additional letters to family in the United States are included in the article above.*

NAS 22 (1965)

Qualey, Carlton C., trans. "Seven America Letters to Valdres," 144–161.

> From: Anders Andersen Qvale, *Muskego, Waukesha County, Wisconsin, 20 October 1850*
> To: Anders Qvale, *Vestre Slidre, Oppland*
> (Nor. ed. I:44, incorrectly dated by Qualey.)

> From: Paul Anderson, *Racine, Wisconsin, 25 November 1851*
> To: Family and friends, *Valdres*
> (Nor. ed. I:58)

> From: Jens and Andreas Tønnesen Skaareland, *Chicago, Illinois, 1 September 1853*
> To: Family and friends, *Aust-Agder*
> (Nor. ed. I:81)

> From: Berit Samsonsdatter Bakken, *Decorah, Winneshiek County, Iowa, 1 August 1869*
> To: Samson Samsonsen and Turi Knudsdatter Bakken, *Vestre Slidre, Oppland*
> (Nor. ed. III:18)

> From: Seborg Samson, *Decorah, Winneshiek County, Iowa, 12 June 1876*
> To: Turid Knutsdatter and Turid Samsonsdatter Bakken, *Vestre Slidre, Oppland*
> (Nor. ed. IV:28)

> From: Anne Samsonsdatter and Ole Olsen Kirkevold, *Adams, Mower County, Minnesota, 14 November 1881*
> To: Turid Knutsdatter and Samson Samsonsen Bakken, *Vestre Slidre, Oppland*
> (Nor. ed. IV:180)

> From: Osten T. Holien, *place unknown, 22 December 1893*
> To: His brother

NAS 23 (1967)

Clausen, C. A., trans. "The Gasmann Brothers Write Home," 71–107.

From: Hans Gasmann, *Pine Lake, Dodge County, Wisconsin, 27 July 1844*
To: Family, *Norway*

From: Hans Gasmann, *Pine Lake, Dodge County, Wisconsin, 20 March 1846*
To: Family, *Norway*

From: Johan Gasmann, *Kristiansand, Vest-Agder, 10 January 1847*
To: Johan Mathias Rye, *Bø, Telemark*
(Nor. ed. I:17)

From: Johan Gasmann, *Appleton, Outagamie County, Wisconsin, 15 December 1855*
To: Johan Mathias and Christiane Elisabeth Rye, *Horten, Vestfold*
(Nor. ed. I:118)

From: Johan Gasmann, *Amherst, Portage County, Wisconsin, November 1860*
To: Johan Mathias Rye, *Horten, Vestfold*
(Nor. ed. II:50)

From: Johan Gasmann, *Amherst, Portage County, Wisconsin, 7 August 1864*
To: Elisa Rye, *Horten, Vestfold*
(Nor. ed. II:112)

NAS 24 (1970)

Hvamstad, Per, trans. "The Letters of Mons H. Grinager: Pioneer Soldier," 29–77.
From: Mons H. Grinager, *25 August 1853, 24 January 1854, 15 May 1854, May 1855, 23 October 1855, 12 July 1856, 16 December 1856, 24 April 1857, 6 July 1859* and *24 May 1862*
To: Family, *Tingelstad, Gran, Oppland*

NAS 27 (1977)

Qualey, Carlton C., trans. "Three America Letters to Lesja," 41–54.

From: Syver Christopherson, *Waseca, Waseca County, Minnesota, 3 October 1869*
To: P. H. Kolstad, *Lesja, Oppland*
(Nor. ed. III:24)

From: Jens Grønbek, *Rice County, Minnesota, 16 September 1867*
To: Christian Heltzen, *Hemnes, Nordland*
(Nor. ed. II:158)

From: Ole, *Duluth, Minnesota, 1896*
To: Family, *Norway*

NAS 28 (1979)

Fletre, Lars, trans. "The Vossing Correspondence Society of 1848 and the Report of Adam Løvenskjold," 245–273.

From: The Vossing Correspondence Society, *Chicago, Illinois, extracts of eight letters dated 30 September 1848 to 1 May 1849*
To: Friends, *Voss, Hordaland*

NAS 32 (1989)

Christianson, J. R., trans. "A Letter of 1852 from Eldorado," 149–156.

From: Bertel Osuldsen, *Eldorado, Fayette County, Iowa, 8 August 1852*
To: Jacob Osuldsen, *Grimstad, Aust-Agder*

INDEXES

SENDERS

Aalvik, Gjert Gjertsen, III:410, 499, 622

Aanonsen, B. G., III:153

Abrahamsen, Jakob, I:96

Allikson, Berent, II:55, 68

Allikson, Berte T., II:55, 91

Allikson, Helena, III:209, 213, 235, 253

Allikson, Rakel Tonette, I:414, II:55, 68, 100

Allikson, Reinert, II:94, 100

Allikson, Siri, II:181, 194, 298, 402, 481; III:81, 193, 217, 224

Andersen, Carl Johan, III:150

Anderson, Elling, II:471

Anderson, Guruanna, II:391, 471, 486

Aslakson, Rakel Tonette, I:341, 346, 392, 403

Aslakson, Reinert, I:165, II:74

Aslakson, Sigbjørn, I:165, 210, 324

Aslakson, Siri/Sara, I:346, 403

Barboe, Gjermund Gjermundsen, I:70

Belle, Haakon Syversen, II:472, 506; III:87

Berby, Inger Hansen, II:450

Bergman, Johan, II:44

Bergman, Kari, II:44

Bjokne, Hans Hansen, II:190, 208, 218, 299, 310, 354, 418, 459, 487

Bjokne, Jacob, III:88

Bjokne, John Hanson, II:337

Bjokne, Jorgen Hansen, II:388; III:66, 88, 105, 203, 224, 243, 257, 575, 616

Bjorli, Amund, II:415, 476

Bjorli, Anne, II:392, 415, 420, 437, 444, 476, 499, 505, 515; III:101, 221, 600

Bjørnsdatter, Torgon, I:113

Bjørnsen, Ellev, I:57, 68, 76, 94, 100

Bjørnsen, Nella, I:118

Bjørnsen, Ole, I:76

Bjørnsen, Torgon, I:100

Blegen, Ingvald, III:323, 354, 615

Blegen, Louis, III:262, 298, 301, 323, 346, 363, 391, 398, 439, 474, 514, 538, 558, 569, 625

Blomqvist, Mina Oline, III:472, 479, 528, 549

Boe, Tarald Guttormsen, III:125

Brager, Karen Olsdatter, II:33, 63, 151

Branson, Hellek G., I:381, 387; II:41, 57, 86, 241, 363

Bringe, Gullik Gulliksen, II:78

Dahl, Christine, II:70, 110, 132, 183, 201, 226, 246, 258, 275, 348, 357, 376, 465

Dahl, Hendrik Olsen, I:402, 426, 454; II:59

Dahle, Knud Halvorsen, I:125

Dahle, Onon Bjørnsen, I:125

Dale, Halvor Halvorsen, III:539

Dale, Ole Havorsen, III:425

Dale, Ole Havorsen, Mrs., III:269

Dilrud, Peder Olsen, II:287
Dorsett, Edvind G., III:352, 471
Dorsett, Gullik Gulliksen, I:85,
99, 115, 242; II:97
Dorsett, Jul/Juul Gulliksen, I:201,
260, 293, 319, 323, 367, 461;
II:40, 62, 373; III:227
Dorsett, Ole Gulliksen, I:85, 99,
201, 260; II:102, 336, 406;
III:352, 366
Dorsett, Susana Halvorsdatter,
I:201
Dybvik, Karl Johan C., III:597

Easthagen, John, III:328
Ellingsen, Ole, III:103
Elsrud, Iver Ellingsen, I:424, 434,
466; II:43, 71, 79, 99, 138, 146,
205, 224, 230, 252, 285, 362,
432; III:169
Elvetun, Nils Ludvigsen, I:183
Enderson, Svend H., II:143, 148,
155, 197, 251, 300, 333, 469;
III:72
Engum, Mary (Marit Wold),
III:263, 268, 271, 273, 275,
280, 291, 297, 300, 316, 321,
345, 368, 385, 402, 407, 417,
436, 449, 483, 552
Erfjord, Sofie, III:620
Erfjord, Svend Svendsen, III:349,
358, 364, 371, 411, 518, 620
Erickson, Martha, II:129, 282,
358, 496
Eriksen, Erik, III:89
Eriksen (Hansen), Inger, II:485;
III:89, 122
Estnes, John, II:540, 585
Evensen, Ingeborg Helgesdatter,
I:444; II:220
Evensen, Ole, I:444; II:220

Feragen, Alex, III:289, 355, 367
Fjære, Kasper Nilsen, III:78
Fjære, Marius, III:586
Fosholt, John Torkelsen, II:334,
342, 365; III:413, 427, 444
Fredriksen, Fredrik J., III:79, 191
Furuset, Anne Pauline
Pedersdatter, II:105, 114, 158

Gamkinn, Hans Nielsen, I:350,
358, 368, 373, 383
Geving, Ole Rasmussen, III:109
Godager, Even Nilsen, II:276
Graven, Gunder Larson, II:46
Gunleiksrud, Gaute Ingebretsen,
I:61, 123, 217, 244, 264; II:109
Gunleiksrud, Kari Sigurdsdatter,
I:217, 244

Hansen, Adolf, III:400
Hansen, Edvard, III:69, 74
Hansen, Jakob, III:152
Hansen, Ragnhild, III:577
Hanson, Gulic, III:313, 490, 525,
541
Hanson, Hagerup, III:458
Hanson, Olianna, II:528
Haugerud, Ole Olsen, the
Younger, I:265, 278, 288, 441;
II:25
Helgelien, Asle K., III:434
Helle, Holger Petterson, I:215
Helseth, Anders Olsen, III:497,
567
Helseth, Anna, III:382
Helseth, Ellen Anna, III:387, 408,
497, 534, 567
Helseth, Jens Olsen, III:378
Henningsen, Hans, III:159
Henriksen, Johan, III:392, 399,
401

Hervin, P. S., III:422
Hestad, Beret Anna, III:387
Heve, Magrete Nilsdatter, I:172, 240, 390
Heve, Ole Olsen, I:172, 240, 390
Hilton, Jacob Hanson, II:164, 175, 223, 228, 260, 266, 268, 288, 304, 331, 410, 448, 468, 558; III:80
Holtseteren, Ole Johansen, I:103, 167, 287, 412
Houg, Halsten, I:420
Houg, Lars Svendsen, I:420
Houg, Svend Larsen, I:140, 153, 168, 198, 251, 283, 335, 420, 446; II:30, 117, 325, 371, 385, 446, 520; III:140
Hove, Magrete Nilsdatter. *See* Heve, Magrete Nilsdatter
Hove, Ole Olsen. *See* Heve, Ole Olsen
Hvashovd, Tosten Levorsen, I:177

Iversen, Ibenhard, III:294, 302, 306
Iversen, Torine, II:338

Jacobson, Christopher, I:188, 262, 299, 431, 455; II:127, 153, 184, 199, 231, 290, 315, 352, 369
Jensen, Anna, III:147
Johnsen, Marius, III:308
Johnson, Larsine, III:496
Johnson, Othelius, III:135
Jørgensen, Arne, II:33, 63, 75, 95

Karlsrud, Ole Stensen, I:80
Killy, Marie J, II:178; III:170, 210, 241, 286, 455, 550, 602
Knudtson, Bergit, III:452
Knudtson, Ole, III:428, 452, 536

Lampland, Marie, III:517
Lande, Ole Gulbrandsen, II:141, 186
Lande, Ole Toreson, II:67
Larsen, Ingeborg, II:393, 549
Larsen, Paul, II:188
Lauransson, Halvor, I:82
Lauransson, Ole, I:82
Lee, Andrew, II:526, 548, 554; III:64, 75, 128, 174, 189, 214, 228, 250
Lee, Anna, II:553; III:138, 251
Lee, Guttorm Olsen, I:308, 377, 428; II:116, 157
Lee, Iver Andersen, II:235, 243, 254, 311, 462, 483, 517, 544; III:206, 245, 277, 380 440, 501, 560, 608
Lee, Mikkel Andersen, II:271, 283, 414, 440, 556; III:230, 375, 415, 459, 530, 570, 605
Lee, Ole Andersen, II:160, 169, 210, 328, 380; III:117, 330
Lee, Ole Olsen, I:377, 458; II:52
Lee, Torgrim Olsen, I:228
Leerfald, John Olsen, II:249, 279, 294
Lehovd, Hellik Olson, I:177, 193, 207, 213, 223, 226, 234, 249, 267, 276, 281, 306, 319, 326, 338, 384, 426; II:150, 167, 340; III:85
Lehovd, Jøran Halvorsdatter, I:394
Lehovd, Ole Olsen, I:306, 330, 338, 363, 394; II:172; III:429
Lehovd, Paul, I:363
Lekve, Brynjulv, I:49
Leren, Peter D., III:63
Lian, Anders Johansen, II:489, 493, 501

Lie, Ole Jørgensen, II:537
Lind, Hans Nilsen, II:421, 475;
    III:194
Lind, Nils, II:407
Lind, Ole, II:407
Lothe, Svein Knudsen, I:47
Løkke, Christian, III:283, 299,
    315, 318, 324, 356, 376, 389,
    393, 438
Løvvold, Hans, III:559

Misten, Andor Jakobsen, III:477
Moen, Eli Helgesdatter, I:443
Moen, Gunder Johnsen, I:443;
    II:193
Myran, Ingrid Helgesdatter, I:290,
    429; II:214
Myran, Ole Aslesen, I:290, 310,
    314, 429; II:214
Myrben, Anund Olsen, III:480,
    546
Møller, Hans E., I:56

Narjord, Ane Kristine
    Tørrisdatter, I:220, 236
Narjord, Elias Hansen, I:190, 204,
    220, 236
Nelson, John, III:469
Nelson, Knute, III:143, 226, 236,
    261, 279, 288, 320, 344, 451
Nelson, N. K., III:580
Nelson, Olaf, III:136, 144, 175,
    182, 201, 218
Nerdrum, Fingar Helgesen, II:81
Nesheim, Lars Nilsen, I:219
Netland, Ole Olsen, III:563
Nilsen, Jens A., II:456
Nilsen, Ole, III:145, 202
Nilsen, Sigri, II:529; III:59, 67
Nohr, Karl, III:591
Nordby, Jens S., III:360, 405, 453

Nordhus, Anne Andresen, II:126
Nordrum, Gunder, II:350, 433
Nordrum, Kari, II:350, 433
Norsby, Anne, II:323, 344, 429,
    455, 477; III:186

Ohnstad, Roggine, III:430
Olsen, Katie, III:157
Olsen, Marie, III:167
Olsen, Nils T. See Olson, Nels/
    Nils T.
Olson, Erick G., III:516, 520, 574
Olson, Ingebrigt H., II:384
Olson, Jacob/Jakob, II:367, 457;
    III:150
Olson, Karen, II:375, 384, 491
Olson, Nels/Nils T., II:202, 217,
    302, 522, 539, III:237, 255,
    395, 494, 522, 542, 564, 572,
    578
Olson, Olianna, II:103
Olson, Rena, II:542, III:229
Opsata, Ole Tollefsen, I:360, 451;
    II:136
Osland, Herbrand Paulsen, I:106,
    182
Osland, Ole Herbrandsen, I:66,
    106
Osuldsen, Peder, III:153

Pedersen, Anders, III:581
Pederson, Martin A., III:433, 467,
    488
Petersen, Edvard, III:537

Rannestad, John Torkelsen, II:131,
    280
Rannestad, Rachel Tonette, II:113,
    181, 555
Reiersen, Ouline, III:111
Renville, Maria J. Killy, II:178

Roe, Nils Tollefsen, I:63
Rogstad, Berger Tollevsen, I:379
Rossing, Ole O., II:248
Rothe, Peter, III:418, 446, 544, 583, 592
Rundhaug, Gulbrand, II:513
Rundhaug, Torgrim Olsen, III:285
Rustand, Ole Hansen, I:231, 259

Sando, Barbro Tollefsdatter, I:316, 349; II:50, 134, 173
Sando, Berthe Maria, II:173
Sando, Ole Eriksen, I:63
Schjøth, Erik Theodor, I:271, 273, 312, 370
Seeberg, Lovise, III:111
Sevathson, Sevath, II:111
Skare, Anders Helgesen, I:203, 225, 314; II:90, 140, 221
Skare, Gunder Helgesen, I:310, 314, 407; II:48
Skare, Ingeborg Helgesdatter, I:290, 310, 314
Skare, Ingrid Helgesdatter, I:153
Skare, Mari Helgesdatter, I:151
Smith, Eli, III:612
Solberg, Christian Edvardsen, III:431, 486, 532, 589
Solberg, Even Edvardsen, III:239, 338, 347, 373, 404, 418, 523, 553, 587, 599, 623
Solberg, Ole Edvardsen, III:456, 466
Solem, Alma, III:526
Solem, Karen, II:389, 412, 427, 442, 461, 466, 490, 507, 511, 534, 540, 560; III:61, 114, 132, 183, 196, 219, 248, 258, 340, 342
Solem, Louis Nilsen, II:320, 355
Solem, Marie, III:475

Solem, Olga, III:478
Songe, Johanne Svenningsdatter, I:186, 208, 211
Spilde, Johannes Iversen, II:480
Steen, John, III:491, 508, 555, 595, 618
Straaberg, H. A., III:325
Svendsen, Nils, III:233
Svendsen, Sigri, III:76, 83, 97, 107, 129, 176, 179, 198, 205, 215, 222
Svenson, John, II:435, 473
Swenson, John, II:360

Taksdal, Ole Jesperson, I:295
Thompson, Osine, III:162
Thorkelson, Rakel Tonnette, II:555; III:252
Thulien, Gulbrand Engebretsen, I:79
Tonning, Jacob, II:122, 124, 399
Torstensen (Vigenstad), Paul, I:462; II:27, 65, 83
Tvede, Elise, I:86
Tønnesen, Ole, III:164

Ulsness, Halvor Hansen, II:377, 439, 510, 546
Urheim, Jacob Larsen, II:321, 524; III:295, 304, 327, 351
Urheim (Utheim), Lars Larsen, II:264. 403
Ursin, Jens Herlef, II:207, 366, 383, 409

Vigenstad, Thor/Thor Torstensen, I:403, 415; II:35, 54, 61, 83
Vike, Knud Ivarson, I:298, 311
Vold, Elling Ellingsen, II:306

RECIPIENTS

Aanonsen, Birgitte L., III:153
Aasland, Hellik Paalsen, I:106, 182
Aasnonsen, Aasine, III:157
Aga, Sjur Knudsen, I:47
Andersen, Ellen, III:160
Aslefet, Knut Gislesen/Gisleson,
 II:172, 340; III:85, 429

Bakken, Anne Vetlesdatter,
 III:480, 522, 546
Bakken, Tor Olsen, II:217, 522;
 III:237, 255, 480
Belle, Syver Olsen, II:472, 506;
 III:87
Berby, Anna Olsen, III:89, 122
Berby, Berthe Marie Sandersdatter,
 II:450, 485
Berby, Hans Olsen, II:450, 485;
 III:89, 122
Bergestua, Edvard Evensen,
 III:239, 338, 347
Bergestua, Marte Rasmusdatter,
 III:239, 338, 347
Bjokne, Jacob H., III:203
Bjøkne, Eli Johannesdatter, II:190,
 208, 218, 299, 310, 337, 354,
 388, 392, 415, 418, 420, 437,
 444, 459, 476, 487, 499, 505,
 515; III:66, 88, 101, 105, 221,
 224, 243, 257, 616
Bjøkne, Hans Jørgensen, II:190,
 208, 218, 299, 310, 337, 354,
 388, 392, 415, 418, 420, 437,
 444, 459, 476, 487, 499, 505,
 515; III:66, 88, 101, 105, 221,
 224, 243, 257, 616

Bjøkne, Mathias Hansen, III:575,
 600
Bjørgum, Johan Henrik Rasmusen,
 II:491; III:63, 109
Bjørnsgard, Marit Hansdatter,
 III:550
Blakkstveit, Ole E., II:205
Bleka, Ingvald Johansen, III:301
Bleka, Johan Jonsen, III:262, 298,
 323, 346, 354, 363, 391, 398,
 439, 474, 514, 538, 558, 569,
 615, 625
Bleka, Matea Larsdatter, III:262,
 298, 323, 346, 354, 363, 391,
 398, 439, 474, 514, 538, 558,
 569, 615, 625
Brendhagen, Johan Olsen, II:75, 95
Brendhagen, Lisbet, II:33, 63, 151
Brusli, Nils Andreas Olsen, II:377,
 439, 510, 546
Bøygaard, Haagen Aslesen, II:111
Bøygard, Guri Tollefsdatter, I:349,
 451; II:136, 173

Daaset, Even Gulliksen, I:367
Daaset, Gullik Evensen, I:85, 99,
 115, 201, 260, 367
Daaset, Torstein/Torsten
 Gulliksen, I:201, 242, 260, 293,
 323, 461; II:40, 62, 97, 102,
 336, 373, 406; III:227, 352,
 366, 471
Dahl, Hendrik Olsen, II:70
Dale, Gunhild Jonsdatter, III:269,
 425

Dale, Jon Halvorsen, III:269, 425, 428, 452, 536, 539
Dannevig, Thomine, I:245, 272, 343, 352, 374, 449; II:37, 87, 215, 295, 307, 339, 346, 396, 424, 452, 502, 551; III:99, 111
Dannevig, Thorvald, I:449; II:497, 533; III:70, 92

Elsrud, Edvard Ellingsen, II:285
Elsrud, Elling Olsen, I:231, 424, 434, 466; II:43, 71, 79, 99, 138, 146, 224, 338; III:169
Elsrud, Gulbrand Ellingsen, II:252
Elsrud, Olea Olsdatter, I:424, 434, 466; II:43, 71, 79, 99, 138, 146, 224; III:169
Elsrud, Ole Ellingsen, II:230
Elsrud, Torgrim Ellingsen, II:334, 342, 365, 513; III:169, 285, 360, 405, 413, 427, 430, 444, 453
Elvetun, Ludvig Kristiansen, I:183
Eriksen, Peder, II:44, 59, 105, 110, 114, 132

Flaten, Marie Helliksdatter, III:517
Furuset, Beate Kristoffersdatter, II:248
Furuset, Erik Pedersen, II:158, 183, 201, 226, 246, 248, 258, 275, 287, 348, 357, 376, 465
Furuset, (Dahl) Peder Eriksen, I:379, 402, 426, 454
Furuset, Siri Kristiansdatter, I:402, 426, 454; II:44, 59, 105, 110, 114, 132, 246, 258, 275, 357

Gamkinn, Niels Jensen, I:350, 358, 368, 373, 383
Geving, Johan Henrik Rasmusen, II:375, 384
Gjestrud, Tora Hansdatter, I:57
Gjestvang, Taale Andreas, I:86, 109, 116, 144, 147
Gjømle, Anders Olsen, II:141, 186
Godager, Even Martinusen, II:276
Gudmundsrud, Aagot Larsdatter, II:529; III:5967, 76, 83, 97, 107, 129, 136, 144, 145, 175, 176, 179, 182, 198, 201, 215, 218, 222, 233
Gudmundsrud, Nils Nilsen, II:529; III:59, 67, 76, 83, 97, 107, 129, 136, 144, 145, 175, 176, 179, 182, 198, 201, 202, 205, 215, 218, 222, 233
Gulovsen, Gulov, I:273
Gundersen, Helge, I:314; II:90, 140
Gunleiksrud, Birgit Gautesdatter, I:61, 123, 264, 428
Gunleiksrud, Hans Ingebretsen, II:109
Gunleiksrud, Ingebret Torsteinsen/ Torstensen, I:61, 123, 217, 244, 264, 428
Gunleiksrud, Kari Sigurdsdatter, I:217
Gustavsen, Jens, III:147

Hansen, Hansine, III:152
Haug, Knud/Knut Larsen, I:168, 198
Haug, Mari Larsdatter, I:168, 198
Haug, Ole Larsen, I:140, 153, 168, 198, 251, 283, 335, 420, 446; II:30, 117, 188, 325, 371, 385, 446, 520; III:140

Lian, Johan Peter Eriksen, II:471, 489, 493, 501, 554; III:174, 214, 228, 250

Liane, Knud Ellingsen, I:58

Lie, Anders Andersen, II:254, 271, 283, 311, 328, 380, 414, 462, 483, 517, 544, 556; III:117, 206, 230, 245, 277, 330, 375, 380, 415, 459, 501, 530, 560, 570, 605, 608

Lie, Anders Olsen, I:228, 308, 377, 438, 458; II:52, 116, 157, 160, 169, 210, 235, 243, 254, 271, 283, 311, 328, 350, 380, 414, 433, 462, 483, 517, 544, 556; III:117

Lie, Kari Mikkelsdatter, II:160, 169, 210, 235, 243, 254, 271, 283, 311, 328, 380

Lie, Mari Olsdatter, II:116, 157

Lie, Ragnild Guttormsdatter, II:311

Liubraaten, Hans Nilsen, II:407

Liubraaten, Helge Kristiansdatter, II:407

Lothe, Elsa Haavardsdatter, II:129, 282, 358, 496

Lothe, Nils Haavardsen, II:358

Løkke, Karl Andreas, III:299, 315, 318, 324, 356, 376, 389, 393

Løkke, Maren Pernille, III:299, 315, 318, 324, 356, 376, 389, 393

Løkke, Martha, III:438

Løkke, Nikolai, III:283

Mikkelsen, Mikke, III:422

Narjord, Hans Pedersen, I:190, 204, 220, 236

Narverud, Ole Andersen, I:66

Nattestadvangen, Edward Evensen. *See* Nøttestadvangen, Edvard Evensen

Nattestadvangen, Marte Rasmusdatter. *See* Nøttestadvangen, Marte Rasmusdatter

Nerdrum, Helge Gundersen. *See* Skare, Helge Gundersen

Neset, Jon Jonsen, III:572

Neset, Svanaug Olsdatter, III:395, 572

Nesheim, Lars Nilsen, I:219

Nesheim, Martha Haldorsdatter, I:172, 240, 390

Nordhus, Peder Mortensen, II:126

Næsheim, Martha Haldorsdatter. *See* Nesheim, Martha Haldorsdatter

Næss, Ansteen Johnsen, I:125

Nøttestadvangen, Edvard Evensen, III:431, 456, 466, 486, 523, 532, 553, 587, 589, 599, 623

Nøttestadvangen, Marte Rasmusdatter, III:431, 456, 466, 486, 523, 532, 553, 587, 589, 599, 623

Oldsdatter, Jørand, II:150

Olsen, Anna Kristine, III:167

Olsen, Ingebret, III:167

Olsen, Johan, II:33, 63, 151

Olsen, Ole, II:103

Opheim, Randi Tollefsdatter, I:349; II:50

Opsata, Haagen Tollefsen, I:360; II:134

Ovedal, Beren/Berent Atlaksen, I:346, 392, 405, 414

Ovedal, Berte Tonette Larsdatter, III:193, 235, 244, 252, 253

Torvetjønn, Gro Oldsdatter, II:539; III:494, 542, 564, 572, 578

Torvetjønn, Ole Olsen, II:202

Tunga, Anlaug Christophersdatter. *See* Tonga, Anlaug Christophersdatter

Tønnesen, Thora, III:164

Vangestad, Ole Nirisen, I:177

Vatland, Svend Samuelsen, III:349, 358, 364, 371, 518, 620

Vatland, Svend Svendsen, III:411

Veen, Matias, III:328

Vigenstad, Ole Torstensen, I:403, 415, 462; II:65, 83

Vigenstad, Paul Torstensen, II:35, 54, 61

Vigenstad, Simen Torstensen, II:27, 83

Vigerus, Ole Olsen, II:367

Vigerust, Marie Olsdatter, II:323, 344, 429, 455, 477, 528, 537, 542, 548, 553; III:64, 138, 150, 186, 189, 229, 251

Vigerust, Mari Olsdatter, III:150, 229

Vigerust, Ragnhild Jakobsdatter, II:103, 367, 457; III:150

Vik, Andrea Marie, III:148

Vik, Kristian Terjesen, III:148

Vik, Sevat Olsen, II:421, 475, III:194

Vike, Dordei Knutsdatter, I:298, 311

Vold, Lisbet L., III:263, 268, 271, 273, 275, 280, 291, 297, 300, 316, 321, 345, 368, 385, 402, 407, 417, 436, 449, 483, 552

Zahl, E.B. Kjerschow, II:207, 366, 383, 409, 456; III:69, 74, 78, 79, 135, 191

Ødegaard, Amalie, II:389, 412, 427, 442, 461, 490, 511, 534, 540, 560; III:61, 114, 132, 219, 258, 340, 342, 475, 478

Ødegaard, Borghild, III:526

Ødegaard, Marie Kristoffersdatter, III:248

Ødegaard, Ole Tobias Olsen, II:320, 355, 389, 412, 427, 442, 461, 507, 534, 540, 560; III:61, 114, 183, 196, 219, 475

Ørstein, Ingebjørg Gulliksdatter/ Hansdatter, III:313, 490, 525, 541

Øverland, Hans Ormsen, I:215

PLACES OF ORIGIN

Abercrombie, North Dakota,
    III:263, 280, 291, 382
Albert Lea, Minnesota, I:278, 288
Alexandria, Minnesota, III:261,
    279, 320, 344
Arctander, Minnesota, II:220
Argyle, Wisconsin, I:368, 373
Ashippun, Wisconsin, I:76, 94,
    100, 113, 118
Astoria, Oregon, III:392, 399, 559
Astoria, South Dakota, III:478,
    526
Audubon, Minnesota, III:297,
    300, 316, 321, 345
Augusta, Georgia, III:228

Badger, Iowa, II:175
Batavia, Illinois, I:188
Belleville, Nevada, II:231, 290,
    315
Belmont, North Dakota, III:125
Black Earth, Dane County,
    Wisconsin, I:228; II:63, 75
Blaine, Idaho, II:393, 399
Blair, Wisconsin, III:269, 425,
    428, 452, 536
Blue Mounds, Wisconsin, I:308
Bodie, California, II:199
Bonners Ferry, Idaho, III:615
Boston, Massachusetts, III:159
Boulder, Colorado, II:223, 228
Bradish, Nebraska, III:577, 591
Brandt, South Dakota, III:114,
    132, 183, 196, 219, 248, 258,
    340, 342, 475

Bratsberg, Minnesota, I:367, 461;
    II:40, 62, 336, 373
Britton, South Dakota, II:375,
    384, 491; III:109
Brooklyn, New York, III:153, 157,
    167, 597
Brownsdale, Minnesota, II:480
Bue, North Dakota, II:392, 415,
    420, 437, 444, 476, 499, 505
Burke, Wisconsin, II:27

Callender, Iowa, II:217, 302, 522,
    539; III:237, 255, 564, 572, 578
Cambridge, Wisconsin, I:172, 240
Camp Mackenzie, Augusta,
    Georgia, III:228
Camp Ramsey, Saint Paul,
    Minnesota, III:214
Carpio, North Dakota, III:433,
    467, 488
Cartwright, North Dakota, III:580
Cerro Gordo, Minnesota, II:181
Chicago, Illinois, I:47, 70, 219;
    II:207, 366, 383, 409, 524;
    III:147, 295, 304, 327, 351
Chippewa Falls, Wisconsin, II:435;
    III:69, 74, 79
Choice, Minnesota, III:227
Christiana, Wisconsin, I:82, 177,
    182, 193, 207, 213, 223, 226,
    234, 249, 276, 281, 306, 319
Clackamas, Oregon, III:490, 525,
    541
Claybank, Minnesota, III:298,
    301, 363
Clifton, Texas, I:454

Hot Creek, Nevada, I:431, 455
Howard, Illinois, I:186, 208, 211

Idaho City, Idaho, I:399
Indian Creek, Leland, Illinois,
    I:85, 99, 115
Island No. 10, Missouri, I:298

Jersey City, New Jersey, III:152
Jewell, Kansas, II:122, 124
Jolon, California, III:472, 479,
    528, 549
Juneau, Alaska, III:389

Kasson, Minnesota, I:363, 394;
    II:172; III:429
Kendall, New York, I:66, 106
Ketchikan, Alaska, III:324
Killisnoo, Alaska, III:306, 356
Koshkonong, Wisconsin, I:58

La Crosse, Wisconsin, III:347
Lake Nebagamon, Wisconsin,
    III:540
Lake Park, Minnesota, II:188
Lakota, North Dakota, II:515;
    III:66, 101, 221
Lanesboro, Minnesota, II:320
Larvik, Vestfold, I:57
Latimore, North Dakota, II:337
Lee, Illinois, II:143, 148, 155
Leeds, Wisconsin, I:462
Leland, Illinois, I:215; II:97, 102,
    406; III:352, 366, 471
Leland Station Illinois, I:242
Liverpool, England, II:489
Locust, Iowa, II:93, 107, 120
Lowry, Minnesota, II:418, 459,
    487, 546; III:88, 105, 203, 224,
    243, 257, 575, 616
Luverne, Minnesota, II:136

Madison, Minnesota, II:280
Madison, Wisconsin, I:183, 330,
    III:418
Manfred, North Dakota, III:349,
    358, 364, 371
Mansfield, South Dakota, III:434
Mantorville, Minnesota, I:267
Marengo, Iowa, II:126
Marlin, Texas, II:54, 61
Mayville, North Dakota, II:483,
    517, 544
Medo, Minnesota, I:414; II:55, 68,
    91, 131
Melville, Montana, III:78, 458,
    577
Milton, North Dakota, II:513
Miner, Wisconsin, III:186
Minneapolis, Minnesota, I:407;
    II:48; III:63, 328, 354
Modena, Wisconsin, II:95, 151
Moorhead, Minnesota, II:276
Moscow, Idaho, II:549
Mount Horeb, Wisconsin, III:330,
    375, 415, 459, 530, 570, 605
Mount Vernon, Wisconsin, II:52,
    160, 169, 235, 440, 556; III:230
Muskego, Wisconsin, I:80, 96
Muskegon, Michigan, I:70

Nacogdoches, Texas, I:86
Nashville, Tennessee, I:311
Necedah, Wisconsin, II:103, 323,
    344, 367, 429, 455, 457, 477,
    528, 537, 542, 548, 553; III:64,
    138, 150, 186, 229, 251
Nerstrand, Minnesota, I:225, 303
Newburg, Minnesota, I:293, 323
New York, New York, I:140;
    III:162, 164
Nielsville, Minnesota, III:560, 608
Norden, North Dakota, II:355

Norden, South Dakota, II:379, 389, 412, 427, 442, 461, 466, 490, 507, 511, 534, 540, 560; III:61

Norman Hill, Texas, I:379, 402, 426

Norse, Texas, II:59, 70, 110, 132, 158, 183, 201, 226, 246, 248, 258, 275, 348, 357, 376, 465

Northwood, North Dakota, II:529; III:59, 67, 76, 83, 97, 107, 129, 176, 179, 198, 205, 215, 222, 233

Norway Hill, Texas, II:287

Norway Lake, Minnesota, I:303, 318, 444; II:193

Norwegian Grove, Minnesota, II:83

Oconomowoc, Wisconsin, I:103, 167

Ogalla, Wisconsin, I:262

Ogdensburg, Wisconsin, III:289, 355, 367

Osakis, Minnesota, II:190

Oslo, Florida, III:387, 408, 497, 534, 565, 567

Oswego, Illinois, I:79

Ottawa, North Dakota, II:334, 365

Paint Creek, Lansing, Iowa, I:119, 159, 162, 180, 195, 256, 300; II:111

Petersburg, Alaska, III:299

Phillips, Wisconsin, III:250

Pine Lake, Lebanon, Wisconsin, I:68

Porsgrunn, Telemark, I:56

Portland, North Dakota, II:462; III:277, 380, 440, 501

Portland, Oregon, III:135, 400, 401, 537, 586

Prairieville, Texas, I:409, 449; II:87, 215, 295, 307, 339, 346, 396, 424, 452, 497, 502, 533, 551; III:92, 99, 111

Presque Isle, Wisconsin, III:516, 520

Primrose, Wisconsin, I:377, 438, 458; II:116, 157

Prospect Bluff, Arkansas, II:83

Radcliffe, Iowa, II:333; III:72

Red Wing, Minnesota, III:346, 439, 474, 514, 538, 558

Reno, Minnesota, II:439

Renville, Minnesota, II:178; III:170, 210, 241, 286

Reynolds, North Dakota, III:103

Rock Creek, Iowa, I:424, 434, 441, 466

Rock Dell, Minnesota, II:340; III:85

Rock Prairie, Wisconsin, I:63

Rothsay, Minnesota, II:350, 433

Rushford, Minnesota, II:264

Sacred Heart, Minnesota, III:455, 550, 602

Saint Ansgar, Iowa, I:231, 259, 360; II:25, 43, 71, 79, 99, 138, 146, 205, 224

Saint Louis, Missouri, I:295

Saint Paul, Minnesota, III:214

Salem, Minnesota, I:326, 338, 384, 436; II:150, 167

Salem, Oregon, II:472, 506; III:87

Salt Lake City, Utah, III:325

San Francisco, California, II:184; III:581

Flesland, Buskerud, I:182
Fræna, Møre og Romsdal, III:378,
   382, 387, 408, 497, 534, 565,
   567

Gausdal, Oppland, I:103, 167,
   287, 412
Gjøvik, Oppland, III:328
Gran, Hadeland, Oppland, I:350,
   358, 368, 373, 383
Granvin, Hordaland, I:172, 219,
   240, 390; II:93, 107, 120, 196,
   480; III:143, 226, 236, 261,
   279, 288, 320, 344, 410, 451,
   499, 504, 622
Grorud, Oslo, III:491, 508

Hamar, Hedmark, II:276
Hedalen, Sør-Aurdal, Oppland,
   I:228, 308, 377, 438, 458; II:52,
   116, 157, 160, 169, 210, 235,
   243, 254, 271, 283, 311, 328,
   350, 380, 414, 433, 440, 462,
   483, 517, 544, 556; III:117, 206,
   230, 245, 277, 330, 375, 380,
   415, 440, 459, 501, 530, 560,
   570, 605, 608
Heddal, Notodden, Telemark,
   I:56, 57, 68, 76, 94, 100, 113,
   118
Heddal, Vang, Hedmark, II:33
Hernes, Bodin, Bodø, Nordland,
   III:283, 299, 315, 318, 324,
   356, 376, 389, 393, 438
Herøy, Møre og Romsdal, II:122,
   124, 399
Hol, Buskerud, III:103
Holt, Tvedestrand, Aust-Agder,
   I:58, 186, 208; III:289, 355,
   367, 516, 520, 574

Jelsa, Suldal, Rogaland, III:349,
   358, 364, 371, 411, 518, 620

Kabelvaag, Vaagan, Nordland,
   III:308
Kautokeino, Finnmark, III:612
Kinsarvik, Ullensvang, Hordaland,
   II:129, 143, 148, 155, 197, 251,
   300, 321, 333, 358, 360, 403,
   435, 469, 473, 496, 524; III:72,
   295, 304, 327, 351, 446, 540,
   585
Kjerringøy, Bodø, Nordland,
   II:207, 366, 383, 409, 456;
   III:69, 74, 78, 79, 135, 193,
   294, 302, 306, 392, 399, 400,
   401, 458, 477, 537, 559, 577,
   580, 586, 591
Kløfta, Ullensaker, Akershus,
   I:188, 262, 399, 431, 455;
   II:260, 266, 268, 288, 290,
   304, 315, 331, 352, 369, 410,
   448, 468; III:80, 558
Kongsberg, Buskerud, I:66

Landvik, Grimstad, Aust-Agder,
   III:156
Lesja, Oppland, II:190, 208, 218,
   299, 310, 337, 354, 388, 392,
   415, 418, 420, 437, 444, 459,
   472, 476, 487, 499, 505, 506,
   515; III:66, 87, 88, 101, 105,
   203, 221, 224, 243, 257, 575,
   600, 616
Lillesand, Aust-Agder, I:245, 272,
   343, 352, 374, 409, 449; II:37,
   87, 215, 295, 307, 339, 346,
   396, 424, 452, 497, 502, 533,
   551; III:70, 111
Løten, Hedmark, I:86, 109, 116,
   144, 147

Madison, Wisconsin, II:35, 54, 61
Møsstrond, Rauland, Vinje,
  Telemark, II:202, 302, 564,
  572, 578, III:395

Nannestad, Akershus, II:320, 355,
  379, 389, 412, 427, 442, 461,
  466, 490, 507, 511, 534, 540,
  560; III:61, 114, 132, 183, 196,
  219, 248, 258, 340, 342, 475,
  478, 526
Nedstrand, Tysvær, Rogaland,
  I:215
Nissedal, Telemark, I:125
Nærbø, Haa, Rogaland, I:295

Os, Hedmark, I:190, 204, 220,
  236
Oslo, I:271, 273, 312, 370;
  III:472, 479, 491, 508, 528,
  549, 555, 581, 595, 618

Rauland, Vinje, Telemark, II:539;
  III:395, 564, 572, 578
Rennesøy, Rogaland, II:126
Ringebu, Oppland, I:79
Romedal, Stange, Hedmark, I:379,
  402, 426, 454; II:44, 59, 70,
  105, 110, 114, 132, 158, 183,
  201, 226, 246, 248, 258, 275,
  287, 348, 357, 376, 465; III:325

Seljord, Telemark, I:82
Settenøy, Vikna, Nord-Trøndelag,
  III:467, 488
Sigdal, Eggedal, Buskerud, II:81,
  90, 407, 421, 475; III:194
Sirdal, Aust-Agder, II:481

Sirdal, Vest-Agder, I:165, 210, 324,
  341, 346, 414; II:55, 68, 74, 91,
  94, 100, 113, 131, 181, 194,
  280, 298, 402, 555; III:81, 193,
  209, 213, 217, 235, 244, 252,
  253
Skatval, Stjørdal, Nord-Trøndelag,
  II:46
Skedsmo, Akershus, I:180, 195,
  256, 300
Solvorn, Luster, Sogn og Fjordane,
  I:183
Songe, Tvedestrand, Aust-Agder,
  I:208, 211
Spring Prairie, Wisconsin, I:298,
  311
Stange, Hedmark, III:422
Stjørdal, Nord-Trøndelag, II:375,
  384, 491; III:63, 109

Tangen, Stange, Hedmark, III:239,
  338, 347, 373, 404, 421, 431,
  456, 466, 486, 523, 532, 553,
  587, 589, 599, 623
Tinn, Telemark, I:61, 80, 96, 123,
  217, 244, 264, 428; II:109
Tretten, Øyer, Oppland, III:262,
  298, 301, 323, 346, 354, 363,
  391, 398, 439, 474, 514, 538,
  558, 569, 615, 625
Trondheim, Sør-Trøndelag,
  III:263, 268, 271, 273, 275,
  280, 291, 297, 300, 316, 321,
  345, 368, 385, 402, 407, 417,
  436, 449, 483, 552
Tønsberg, Vestfold, III:92, 99, 111
Tørdal, Drangedal, Telemark,
  II:377, 439, 510, 546

BIOGRAPHICAL NAMES

Aabel, Mrs., I:356

Aaberg, Ole, III:361

Aaberlus, Mr., I:127–128, 132–133

Aaboen, A., III:66

Aagot, Miss, III:514, 557, 619

Aalde, Marie, II:80

Aall, Dicta (Elise Benedicte), II:397, 425, 426; III:94

Aall, Jacob, II:425, 426, 453, 454

Aalvik, Gjert Gjertsen, III:410–411, 501, 622–623

Aalvik, Ole Gjertsen, III:501, 623

Aamodt, Karen, II:390

Aamotstuen, Karen, II:467

Aandalskaret, Marie, III:535

Aanesruddalen, Dorthea, II:512, 541

Aanonsen. *See also* Andersen

Aanonsen, B. G., III:156

Aanonsen, Birgitte L., III:153

Aanonsen, Aasine, III:157–158

Aarhus, Lars Olsen, III:410, 622

Aarstøl, Nils, III:469, 470

Aarstøl, Thomas Tobiassen, III:470

Aas, Albertine, III:386

Aas, Carl, I:162, 257, 257, 258, 301, 302

Aas, Christine Carlsdatter. *See* Drue, Christine Carlsdatter

Aas, Mari Olsdatter, I:197, 258

Aas, Martha, II:348

Aas, Torine, I:258

Aasen, Ivar, III:448, 449, 584

Aasen, Per, II:227

Aasildrud, Ingebor/Ingeborg Halvorsdatter, I:69, 102

Aasland, Hellik Paalsen, I:106, 107, 182–183

Aasland, Knut, III:470

Aaslandeie, Ole, I:177

Aasleggen, Hellik Andersen, I:179

Aasmundsdatter, Anne, II:218

Aavedahl/Aavedal. *See* Allikson; Aslakson; Ovedal

Abrahamsen, Gro Gjermundsdatter, I:96, 97, 98

Abrahamsen, Jakob, I:96–97, 98

Abrahamsen, Thomas, I:96

Acker, Nils, III:262, 440

Acker, Oline, III:440

Afdem, Ole, III:225

Aga, Sjur Knudsen, I:47

Akerhaugen, Halvor Halvorsen, I:76, 78, 114

Albertine, Elise. *See* Henriksen, Elise Albertine

Albertson, Elef, I:246, 248

Allen, Hans, II:518, 520

Alliksen. *See* Allikson

Allikson. *See also* Aslakson; Ovedal

Allikson, Alexander Sigbjørnsen, III:217

Allikson, Berent/Bernt Andreas, II:55–56, 68–69, 74, 92, 481, 482; III:81, 193, 253

Allikson, Berte Tonette, II:55–56, 69, 91–92, 131, 181, 182, 195, 298, 402, 403, 481, 482, 556; III:253

Arentz/Arenz, Thomine, I:355;
II:552
Arndt, Johann, I:252, 254; II:556
Arneberg, Ole, II:466
Arnelien, Tollef, III:108
Arnesen, Haagine Johnsdatter,
I:258
Arnesen, Hans, I:258
Arntzen, Sine, I:356, 411; II:89
Asbjørnsen, Erik, III:82
Asche, Frederic/Frederick (Oluf
Frithjof), II:229, 230, 289, 304,
305, 353, 354
Asche, Fritjof/Frithjof, II:230,
262, 267, 268, 288
Asche, Thomas, II:230, 262
Ask, Mrs., III:134
Aslagedatter/Aslagsdatter. See
Allikson; Aslakson; Ovedal/
Ovedahl
Aslagsen/Aslagson. See Allikson;
Aslakson; Ovedal/Ovedahl
Aslaksdatter. See Allikson;
Aslakson; Ovedal/Ovedahl
Aslaksen, Gunder, I:209
Aslakson. See also Allikson;
Ovedal
Aslakson, Alexander, I:325
Aslakson, Berthe, I:325
Aslakson, Rakel/Rachel Tonette,
I:341–342, 347, 393–394, 405,
406
Aslakson, Sara Atlaksdatter, I:347,
393, 394, 406, 407, 414; II:55,
95, 101, 113
Aslakson, Sivert, I:166, 210, 324,
325, 341, 346, 392, 406; II:56,
69, 74
Asle, Enger, II:72, 73
Aslefet, Jørand Olsdatter, II:150,
167–168

Aslefet, Knut Gislesen/Gisleson,
II:172–173, 340–341; III:85–
86, 429
Aslesen, Haagen. See Bøygaard,
Haagen Aslesen
Aslesen, Hellik, I:386
Aslesen, Ole. See Myran/Myrand,
Ole Aslesen
Asplund, Professor, II:288, 290
Assorsdatter, Ingrid, I:171
Atlagdatter/Atlagsdatter. See
Allikson; Aslakson; Ovedal/
Ovedahl
Atlagsen/Atlagson. See Allikson;
Aslakson; Ovedal/Ovedahl
Atlaksdatter/Atlakson. See
Allikson; Aslakson; Ovedal/
Ovedahl
Attlagdatter/Attlagsdatter. See
Allikson; Aslakson; Ovedal/
Ovedahl
Ausen, Gulbrand, I:189
Austrem, Tollag, III:81

Baardsen, Beruld, I:74, 75
Baardsen, Jens, II:382
Bache, Edward, I:410
Bache, Erik/Erick, I:109, 111, 246,
248, 375
Bache, Ingeborg, I:246, 248, 375,
377
Bache, Mrs., I:376, 410–411, 449,
450; II:37, 38, 39; III:92–93.
See also Pabst, Ingeborg
Bache family, I:354
Bagaas, Knut, II:408, 409
Bagge, Henrik, II:230, 231
Baglien, Erik, III:181
Bak/Bakk, Ingebrikt, III:292
Bak/Bakk, Kari, III:292

Bak/Bakk, Randi, III:272, 293, 386, 437

Bakke, Aslaug, II:406

Bakke, Even, II:29; III:256

Bakken, Andreas, II:368

Bakken, Anne Vetlesdatter, II:523; III:237, 480, 483, 494, 495, 522–523, 546, 565

Bakken, Jørgen, II:368

Bakken, Tor/Thor Olsen, II:204, 217–218, 522–523, 539, 540; III:237, 255–256, 480, 483, 494, 495, 523, 565

Bakkom, H., I:460

Bakli, Bol, I:437

Baklien, Anders, III:108, 182–183

Baklien, Turi, III:108

Bakos, Ole, I:191

Bangsjordet, Halvor, II:273

Barboe, Gjermund Gjermundsen, I:75

Barlien, Hans, I:340

Barron, Andrew Cornelius, III:601, 617

Barskrind, Erik Kittilsen, I:65; II:134

Barstad, Peder Hansen, I:393

Basberg, Anton, I:357

Basberg, Else, I:353, 357, 411

Basberg, Frederik, I:357

Basberg, Mrs., I:353, 354, 357, 411; II:89, 347, 397, 425, 426, 452

Bastholm, Christian, I:54, 55

Bekkestad, Erling T., III:203, 215, 216

Belgum, Gunhild/Gunnild, II:212, 240, 241; III:120, 464

Belgum, Syver Nilsen, II:212, 240, 328; III:120

Belle, Blanche, II:473; III:87

Belle, Brit, III:87

Belle, Claude, II:473, 507; III:87

Belle, Eugenia, III:87

Belle, Haakon Syversen, II:472–473, 506–507; III:87

Belle, Lelah, II:507

Belle, Syver/Syvert Olsen, II:472–473, 506–507; III:87

Belsby, Ole Sandersen, II:451; III:90, 92

Bendiksen, Mr., III:409

Benedicte, Elise (Dicta Aall), II:426

Benneche, Lovise, I:375

Benson, Bennet A., III:617

Berby, Anna Hansen, II:451; III:123, 124

Berby, Berte/Berthe/Bertha Marie Sandersdatter, II:450–451, 485; III:92, 124

Berby, Hans Olsen, II:450–451, 485; III:89, 92, 122

Berby, Inger Hansen/Hansdatter, II:450–451; III:89, 92. *See also* Eriksen, Inger

Berenhard, Hans, I:78, 95

Berg, Ann, III:336

Berg, Frederick R., I:299

Berg, Gulborg/Gullborg O., II:117, 163

Berg, Gulbrand, I:228

Berg, Halvor Knudsen, I:396

Berg, Kari, II:421; III:102

Berg, Ole Vetlesen, I:245; II:109

Berge, Gunild Pedersdatter, I:97

Berge, Halvor Torgrimsen, I:97

Berge, Karoline, III:535

Berge, Knut, II:264

Berge, Torje, III:355

Bergene, Ingeborg, II:483

Bergene, Ingrid, II:312

Bergene, Ole, III:531, 572
Berger, I., III:115
Berger, Lars, III:184
Berger, Ole, II:467
Bergersen, Gunder, III:474
Bergersen, Helene, III:479, 480
Bergersen, Severin, III:474, 529, 582
Bergerud, Ambjørg, I:322
Bergerud, Anders, III:208
Bergerud, Anund, I:250
Bergerud, Beret, I:382
Bergerud, Hellik, I:180, 322
Bergerud, Tosten, I:182
Bergesen, Gustav Martin, III:535
Bergesen, Ivrikka, III:534, 535
Bergestua, Edvard/Evard Evensen, III:239–240, 338, 347
Bergestua, Marte Rasmusdatter/Rasmussen, III:239–240, 338, 347
Berget, Jøran Sjulsdatter, I:234
Berget, Kari, II:58
Bergman, Johan, II:44–45, 110, 111
Bergman, John, II:59, 60
Bergman, Kari, II:44–45, 59–60, 110, 111, 247, 259
Bergrud, Beret, I:333
Bergsland, Halvor, I:84
Berket, Mr., II:242
Bernhard, Albert, II:181
Bernhoft, Adam, III:300, 319, 389–390, 394
Bernhoft, Olaf, III:300, 319, 325, 389–390, 394
Bersangaard, Ole, II:553
Berte, Anne, I:347–348
Berteusen, Norman, III:309, 312
Bertilrud, Gulbrand, III:248
Bertilrud, Iver, II:517

Bertilrud, Kari, II:434, 463
Bertilrud, Syver, III:562, 609
Bertilrud family, II:463, 483, 518–519
Bertine, Karen, II:481, 482, 555, 556; III:82, 193
Bervig, Osmund, III:364
Bidsler, Johan, II:443
Bidsler, Marthea, II:443
Bidsler boys, II:443
Birch, Paul Hansen, General, I:116
Birkaaker, Trond, III:266
Bitøen, Ingeborg, I:54
Bjerke, Nina, III:341, 343
Bjerkeg, Kari, II:389
Bjerkeg, Kristoffer, II:389
Bjerkgaarden, Anund Hansen, I:382
Bjerkgaarden, Ole, I:382
Bjokne/Bjøkne. See also Bjorli
Bjokne/Bjøkne, Edvard, III:257
Bjokne/Bjøkne, Eli Johannesdatter, II:190, 208–209, 218–219, 299–300, 310–311, 337–338, 354–355, 388–389, 392–393, 415, 418–419, 420–421, 437–438, 444–445, 459–460, 476–477, 487–488, 499–500, 505–506, 515–516; III:66–67, 88–89, 101–102, 105–106, 221, 224, 243–244, 257–258
Bjokne/Bjøkne, Guri/Guro Johannesdatter, II:419, 445, 488, 505. See also Justen, Guro
Bjokne/Bjøkne, Hans Hansen, II:192, 208–209, 218–219, 299–300, 310–311, 354–355, 388, 389, 418–419, 459–460, 487–488; III:88, 244

Bjokne/Bjøkne, Hans Jørgensen,
II:190, 208–209, 218–219,
299–300, 310–311, 337–338,
354–355, 388–389, 392–393,
415, 418–419, 420–421,
437–438, 444–445, 459–460,
476–477, 487–488, 499–500,
505–506, 515–516; III:66–67,
88–89, 101–102, 105–106, 221,
224, 243–244, 257–258
Bjokne/Bjøkne, Ida H., III:617
Bjokne/Bjøkne, Jacob/Jakob
Hansen, II:192, 515, 516;
III:66–67, 88–89, 203–204,
225–226, 257–258, 577, 617
Bjokne/Bjøkne, Johannes/John
Hanson, II:191, 192, 310, 311,
337–338, 355, 388, 392, 393,
419, 421; III:67
Bjokne/Bjøkne, Jorgen/Jørgen
Hansen, II:192, 355, 388–389,
392, 419, 420, 421, 445, 460,
488, 500, 516; III:66, 67,
88–89, 105–106, 203–204,
225, 243–244, 257, 616–617
Bjokne/Bjøkne, Kari Berntsdatter,
III:66, 67, 88, 89
Bjokne/Bjøkne, M., III:88
Bjokne/Bjøkne, Mari, II:190, 445
Bjokne/Bjøkne, Marit, II:219, 284,
299, 300, 337–338, 389, 460,
515, 516
Bjokne/Bjøkne, Mathias/Matias/
Mattias Hansen, II:420, 421,
438, 487, 488, 500, 515;
III:224, 225, 243, 575, 600–
601
Bjokne/Bjøkne, Ole, II:208, 506;
III:225
Bjokne/Bjøkne, Ole Jørgensen,
II:445, 488

Bjokne/Bjøkne, Rønnaug
Hansdatter, II:421
Bjokne/Bjøkne, Tosten, III:225
Bjork, Kenneth O., II:263
Bjorli. See also Bjokne/Bjøkne
Bjorli, Amund Pedersen, II:192,
392–393, 415–416, 417, 418,
420–421, 438, 444, 445,
476–477, 499, 500, 506, 516;
III:66, 67, 101, 102, 225, 617
Bjorli, Anne, II:192, 219,
392–393, 417, 418, 420–421,
437–438, 444–445, 476–477,
499–500, 505–506, 515–516;
III:66, 67, 101–102, 221, 244,
577, 600–601, 617
Bjorli, Elise, II:515–516; III:102
Bjorli, Ingri, II:500
Bjorli, Jøda, II:500
Bjorli, Knut, II:417, 418, 438, 445
Bjorli, Lars Pedersen, II:392, 445;
III:601
Bjorli, Peder Engebretsen, II:393,
417, 418, 438, 476, 477
Bjorlivold, Ole, II:392
Bjorlivold, Syver, II:392
Bjornerud/Bjørnrud, Ole, II:408,
422, 475
Bjornerud/Bjørnrud, Turi, II:408
Bjotvet, Halvor, II:145–146
Bjotvet, Sigri, II:145–146
Bjukn. See Bjøkne
Bjøkne. See Bjokne/Bjøkne
Bjørgum, Johan Henrik
Rasmusen/Rasmussen, II:491–
492; III:63–64, 109, 110. See
also Geving, Johan Henrik
Rasmusen
Bjørgum, Magnus, II:492
Bjørgum, Torsten, II:492
Bjørkelid, Ole, III:470

Bjørkerud, Kristofer, II:221
Bjørktuft, Aslaug Sigurdsdatter,
   I:124
Bjørktuft, Jacob Torgrimsen, I:96
Bjørnejordet, Harald, II:547
Bjørnersdatter, Ingeborg, II:345
Bjørnersen, Jakob, II:345
Bjørnsen. *See also* Bjørnson
Bjørnsen, A. *See* Dahle, Onon
   Bjørnsen
Bjørnsen, Adolf Oscar, I:95, 102
Bjørnsen, Anlaug
   Christophersdatter, I:56, 57,
   113
Bjørnsen, Ellev, I:56, 57, 69–70,
   78–79, 94–95, 102, 113, 114,
   118–119. *See also* Tangen, Ellev
   Bjørnsen
Bjørnsen, Halvor, I:69, 94,
   114. *See also* Tonga, Halvor
   Bjørnsen
Bjørnsen, Hans, I:102
Bjørnsen, Mathias, I:114
Bjørnsen, Nella, I:95, 118–119
Bjørnsen, Ole, I:76–79, 94–95, 102
Bjørnsen, Otto, I:102
Bjørnsen, Peter, III:64
Bjørnsen, Sergeant H., II:423
Bjørnsen, Torgon, I:76, 77, 78, 94,
   95, 101, 102, 113–114, 118–119
Bjørnsgard, Marit Hansdatter,
   III:550–551
Bjørnson. *See also* Bjørnsen
Bjørnson, Bjørnstjerne, II:425,
   426, 498, 499; III:93, 96, 236,
   509, 592, 594
Bjørtuft, Aslaug Sigurdsdatter,
   I:124, 125, 218
Bjørtuft, Kittil, I:218
Blakkestad, Ingeborg Tollefsdatter,
   I:65

Blakkestad, Lars Torsen, I:65
Blakkestad, Ole Torsen, I:65
Blakkstveit, Ole E., II:205
Blegen. *See also* Bleka
Blegen, Anders/Andrew
   Engebretsen, I:351–352, 359,
   383
Blegen, Gulbrand, I:368
Blegen, Ingvald, III:301–302, 323,
   346, 354, 391, 398, 439–440,
   475, 615–616
Blegen, Johannes, III:346–347,
   354, 363, 391, 398, 440, 558,
   559
Blegen, Klara, III:440, 475, 538,
   616
Blegen, Kristina, III:391, 440, 515,
   538, 616
Blegen, Kristine, III:475
Blegen, Louis/Laurits, III:262–
   263, 298, 301–302, 323,
   346–347, 354, 363, 391, 398,
   439–440, 474–475, 514–515,
   538, 558–559, 569–570, 616,
   625–626
Blegen, Ole Engebretsen, I:351,
   370
Blegen, Theodore C., I:323; II:532
Blegen, Tilda, III:391, 440, 559
Blegstad, Mrs., II:535; III:185,
   196, 197, 219–220
Blegstad, Ole, III:185–186, 196,
   197, 219–220, 340
Bleie, Ole Samsonsen, I:47
Bleie, Willich Olsen, I:47
Bleka. *See also* Blegen
Bleka, Ingvald Johansen, III:301–
   302

Bleka, Johan Jonsen, III:262–263, 298, 323, 346–347, 354, 363, 391, 398, 439–440, 474–475, 514–515, 538, 558–559, 569–570, 615–616, 625–626

Bleka, Mathea/Matea Larsdatter, III:262–263, 298, 323, 346–347, 354, 363, 391, 398, 439–440, 474–475, 514–515, 538, 558–559, 569–570, 615–616, 625–626

Blekke, Gulbrand, III:249

Blekke, Jens, II:380

Blekke, Martha, III:249

Blessum, Hans, I:463, 465; II:29

Blessum, Simon, I:465; II:29

Blikfeldt, Mr., I:108

Blomqvist, John A., III:473, 550

Blomqvist, Mina Oline, III:473–474, 479–480, 529–530, 549–550, 582

Bloug, Hilda, III:169

Boe/Bøe/Bø, Liv G., III:127

Boe/Bøe/Bø, Martin, III:291, 370

Boe/Bøe/Bø, Tarald Guttormsen, III:127

Boe/Bøe/Bø, Tore, III:266, 291, 370

Bolsøy, Anna, III:566

Bondies, Georg, I:92

Bonli, Ole, I:229

Botten, Morten, III:204

Bottolfsen, Bottolf, I:258

Bottolfsen, Maren, I:258, 302

Bottolfsen, Nils, I:258, 302

Boyum, Arne E., I:253, 255

Braata, Amund, I:364

Braata, Anund Anundsen/Anunsen, I:213, 224, 249

Braata, Tosten Anunsen, I:224, 277

Braaten, Karen Svenningsdatter, I:209

Braaten, Lars, III:200

Braaten, Maret Amundsdatter, I:234

Braaten, Narve, I:361

Braaten, Ole G., III:361

Braaten, Svenning A., I:186, 209

Braathen. *See* Braaten

Brager, Anders, I:460

Brager, Arne Jørgensen, II:34, 65, 77, 97

Brager, Christopher, II:272

Brager, Gunhild Amalie, II:34, 64, 76, 96–97

Brager, Halsten, I:378, 379

Brager, Johan Albert, II:76, 96–97

Brager, Karen Olsdatter, II:34–35, 65, 76, 77, 96–97, 151–152

Brager, Ole, I:228

Brager, Petter, II:273

Bragerhaugen, Harald, III:609

Brakahagen, Kari Olsdatter, I:230

Brandli, Andreas, II:506

Brandli, Matthias/Matias Niklasen, II:392, 393, 506

Brandt, Kristian, II:278

Brandt, Nils Olsen, I:158; II:76, 77, 427, 428; III:116, 197, 507

Brandt, Realf Ottesen, II:428, 467; III:116

Branson, Gulbrand Helliksen, I:381, 382, 388, 389; II:42

Branson, Harry, I:388

Branson, Hellek/Hellik G., I:382, 389; II:41–42, 58–59, 68, 86–87, 242–243, 363–364

Branson, Henry, I:388; II:42, 242, 364

Branson, Margaret Helliksdatter, I:382; II:42

Branson, Ole, I:381, 387–388
Branson, Sam, II:364
Brant. *See* Brandt
Bratager/Brattegard, Ole Person, I:252, 255
Bratlien, Oliv Halvorsdatter, I:380, 381
Bratrud, Oline, III:562
Bredesen, A., II:211
Bredstue, Ole, II:278
Brekhus, Edward, III:171, 173
Brekke, Nils, III:336
Brenden, Anders Olsen, II:441
Brenden, Anne, II:434
Brenden, Iver A., II:434, 441
Brenden, Kari Berntsdatter, III:66, 67
Brenden, Olaug, II:351, 435
Brenden, Ole, II:284
Brenden, Petra, III:257
Brændhagen. *See* Brendhagen/ Brændhagen
Brendhagen/Brændhagen, Johan Olsen, II:33, 63, 75, 95, 96, 151–152
Brendhagen/Brændhagen, Lisbet/ Lisbeth, II:33, 63, 151–152
Bringa, Gunhild, I:83
Bringa, Knut, I:83
Bringe, Gullik Gulliksen, I:382, 383, 388, 389, 395; II:42, 57–58, 78–79, 87, 186, 187, 242, 364
Bringe, Kari Gulbrandsdatter, I:382, 383, 389; II:42
Bringe, Ragnhild, II:57–58
Brodahl, Peder Marius, I:378–379
Brok, Gunder T., III:126
Brokke, Saave, III:126
Brorson, Hans Adolph, II:387
Brotnu, Mr., I:400

Brovold, Mattis, II:436
Brovold, Sigri, II:436
Brown, C. H., I:320
Brubraaten, Ole, II:72
Brunbakke, Elling, II:31
Brunbakke, Ole, II:31
Brunstad, Anne Eriksdatter, I:380, 455; II:106, 116
Brunstad, Annie, II:106
Brunstad, Christine, I:454, 455
Brunstad, Gine, II:105, 106, 276
Brunstad, Gudbrand, II:115
Brunstad, Johan, I:148, 150, 380, 455; II:106, 116
Brunstad, Margrete, I:149, 150
Brunstad, Ole, I:454, 455; II:70, 105, 106, 276
Brunstad family, I:144
Bruseli, A. O. *See* Brusli, Nils Andreas Olsen
Bruskerud, Marie, II:544
Brusli, Gunhild Johanne Nilsdatter/Nillie, II:378, 440
Brusli, Nils Andreas Olsen, II:377, 378, 439–440, 510–511, 546–547
Bryan, William Jennings, III:174, 261
Bryn, Helmer Halvorsen, III:613, 615
Bryni, Anders, II:60, 377
Bryni, Anton, II:183, 184, 247
Bryni, Marte/Marthe, II:288, 377
Brøste, Guro, II:417, 419
Buan, Ole-Hans, III:355
Buchanan, James, President, I:250
Budde, Carl, I:353, 355, 357, 450
Buin, Berit Julsdatter, I:213
Buin, Ingebør Thoresdatter, I:249
Buin, Ole Amundsen, III:85
Buin, Tallef, I:437

Buk, Christen Olsen, I:238

Bursum, Olaf, II:410, 412

Buschmann, August B., III:315, 316, 319, 394

Buschmann, Christ., III:315

Buschmann, Peter T., III:284–285, 299, 319, 325, 394

Busemoen, Taran, II:284, 285

Busemoen, Østen, II:284, 285

Busteraak, Aase, II:378, 439

Busumoen, Gulbrand, II:312

Busumoen, Ole, II:312

Butler, General, I:299

Bye, Ellev, II:294

Byttingsrud, Torvald, I:425

Bø/Bøe. *See* Boe/Bøe/Bø

Bøckmann, Egil, II:496, 497

Bøle, Ole, II:240

Børtnes, Andreas, II:213, 240; III:248, 337, 416

Børtnes, Eric/Erik, II:213, 240, 483, 484; III:442

Børtnes, Halsten/Hallsten Halstensen/Hallstensen, II:53, 162, 164, 212, 213, 240, 258, 274; III:337

Børtnes, Iver, II:211, 314, 483, 484, 517; III:337

Børtnes, Martha N., II:464

Børtnes, Olaug. *See* Eriksen, Olaug Børtnes

Børtnes, Olea Olsdatter, I:290, 379, 440–441, 460; II:53, 117, 164, 213, 258, 274, 314, 442; III:121, 376, 572

Børtnes, Ole Halstensen, II:53, 162, 164, 211, 212, 213, 240, 274, 382, 383, 464; III:336, 415, 416, 442, 571, 572, 607

Børtnes boys, I:459, 460; II:212–213, 464

Børve, Osmund, II:145

Børven, Knud Olsen, I:47

Bøygard/Bøygaard, Guri Tollefsdatter, I:317, 349–350, 451; II:51, 135, 136, 173

Bøygard/Bøygaard, Haagen Aslesen, II:111–112

Campbell, Captain, III:389

Canuteson. *See also* Knudsen; Knudtson; Knutsen

Canuteson, Annie Mathilda, II:106

Canuteson, Ole, III:99, 100, 101

Carl, King, III:380

Carlsen, Johan, III:394

Carlson, Fredrick Herman, II:33

Carl XV, King, II:277

Carranza, President, III:619

Casberg. *See also* Kasberg

Casberg, Carl, III:486, 487

Casberg/Kasberg, Laura. *See* Solberg, Laura

Casper, Gotfred, II:359

Chandler, Mrs., I:462

Christensen. *See also* Christiansen; Kristensen

Christensen, A., I:159–160, 164

Christensen, Mr., II:246

Christensen, Pastor, III:613

Christensen, Søren, I:64

Christian, Peder, I:347–348

Christiansen. *See also* Christensen; Kristiansen

Christiansen, Mrs., II:289

Christoffersen. *See also* Christophersen; Christopherson

Christoffersen, Halvor, I:359

Christopher, Amund, I:299

Christophersen. *See also* Christoffersen; Christopherson

Christophersen, Nils, II:321
Christophersen, Ole, II:560, 562
Christopherson. *See also*
Christoffersen; Christophersen
Christopherson, Maria, II:442,
443, 462
Claghorn, C., III:158
Clark, Champ, III:557, 558
Clausen, Clarence A., I:248
Clausen, Claus Lauritz, I:98, 156,
158, 168–169, 171, 200, 299,
361–362, 420–421, 435, 446,
452; II:27; III:507
Clausen/Claussen, Olaf/Ollof A.,
III:375, 416
Cleveland, Grover, President,
II:374; III:121–122
Collett, Camilla, II:425, 426
Collett, Mr., I:108
Colwick, Martha, II:276
Colwick, Mr., II:276
Colwick, O., II:70
Cook, Mr., I:88
Crosby, Mr., II:177, 178
Crøger, Mr., I:246

Daaset. *See also* Dorsett
Daaset, Even Gulliksen, I:99, 367;
II:103
Daaset, Gullik Evensen, I:85–86,
99–100, 115–116, 201–202,
260–261, 367
Daaset, Hellik, II:103, 407; III:353
Daaset, Torsten/Torstein/
Thorsten/Tostein/Tosten
Gulliksen/Gullekson, I:201–202,
242–243, 260–261, 293–294,
323–324, 461–462; II:40–41,
62–63, 97–98, 102–103, 186,
336, 373–374, 406–407;
III:227, 352–53, 366, 471

Daaseth/Daasett. *See* Dorsett;
Daaset
Dahl. *See also* Dahle; Dal
Dahl, Anders, I:426; II:377
Dahl, Caroline, II:59, 60; II:59,
60, 70–71, 376
Dahl, Christine, I:144, 147,
381, 403, 426, 427, 454–455;
II:45, 59, 60, 70–71, 105, 106,
110–111, 115, 133–134, 158,
183–184, 201–202, 226–227,
247–248, 258–259, 275–276,
287–288, 348–349, 357–358,
376–377, 465–466
Dahl, Gine, I:402, 403; II:376,
377
Dahl, Hans, II:133
Dahl, Hendrick Olsen, I:144,
147, 380, 381, 402–403, 427,
454–455; II:45, 59–60, 70–71,
105, 106, 110, 115, 116
Dahl, N. P., I:271
Dahl, Ole, I:454; II:71, 133, 134,
183–184, 201, 288, 348; III:254
Dahl, Otto, II:259
Dahl, Syverine, I:454; II:111, 115,
133, 134, 159, 183, 184, 201,
226, 259, 276, 349, 376, 377
Dahl, Wenche, II:89; III:94
Dahle. *See also* Dahl; Dal
Dahle, Knud Halvorsen, I:129–
130, 133–134, 136, 139, 366,
398
Dahle, Onon Bjørnsen, I:139
Dal, Ole H., II:259
Dala, Kirsti, I:238
Dale, Genilie/Genelie/Gunhild,
III:270–271
Dale, Gunhild Jonsdatter, III:269,
425–426, 453, 540

Dale, Halvor Halvorsen, III:539–540

Dale, Jon/John Halvorsen, III:269, 425–426, 428–429, 452–453, 536, 539–540

Dale, Lars, III:271

Dale, Ole/Ola Halvorsen, III:270–271, 425–426, 429, 536, 540

Dalen, Jakob/Jacob, II:430; III:204

Dalen, Johannes, II:355

Dalen, Mrs., III:204

Damholt, Henrik, II:170

Danielsen, Henrik, III:400

Dannevig, Lars Tellefsen, I:345; II:90

Dannevig, Niels, I:272, 273, 353, 375, 449; II:37, 40, 90, 308, 552

Dannevig, Thomine, I:245–248, 272–273, 343–345, 352–357, 449–450; II:37, 39, 40, 87, 90, 215–216, 295, 297, 307, 339–340, 346, 396–398, 424, 452, 454, 455, 502, 504, 505, 551–552; III:99, 101, 112–113

Dannevig, Thorvald, I:246, 247, 272–273, 343, 345, 352, 354, 355, 374–377, 411, 449–450; II:39, 88–89, 216, 295, 308, 340, 346, 348, 424, 425, 453, 497–499, 533, 552; III:70, 92, 100, 112, 113

Dannevig, Vilhelmine, II:40, 90

Darius, III:596, 597

Daset, Ole G. See Dorsett, Ole Gulliksen

Dass, Petter, I:270

Debs, Eugene, III:340

Dederiksøn, Mr., I:209

Dedriksøn, Pastor. See Dietrichson, Gustav Fredrik

Dehli, Engebret Larsen, I:123

Dehli, Lars, I:123

Dehli, Peder, I:123

Dehli boys, I:120, 121, 123

Dengerud, T., II:531

Didrichsen, Kristiane, III:315, 316, 319

Dietrichson, Gustav Fredrik, I:186, 187, 209, 210, 211

Dietrichson, J. W. C., I:55, 62, 83, 84, 104, 105, 177, 216, 217

Dille, Peder Abrahamsen, I:238

Dillerud. See Dilrud

Dilrud, Gine, II:114, 115–116

Dilrud, Karen, II:106, 110, 114, 115, 158, 159, 201, 247, 248, 259, 288, 349, 357, 376, 465, 466

Dilrud, Peder/Peter/Per Olsen, II:106, 110, 115, 133, 183, 226, 227, 247–248, 259, 275, 287–288, 349

Dokken, Elling Tostensen, II:326, 327, 373, 521, 522; III:143

Dokken, Gulbrand Toreson, I:227, 321

Dokken, Ingebør Toresdatter, I:234

Dokken, Ingri, II:373

Dokken, Ingrid, II:447, 521, 522; III:143

Dokken, Julia Oline, I:321

Dokken, Nils, I:199

Dokken, Ragnil, II:522

Dokkhaugen, G., I:460

Dokkmyrane, Margit Eivindsdatter, I:200

Dokkmyrane, Ole Olsen, I:199, 200

Dolven, Ole, I:229, 230, 308

Domstadskjæret, Ingebret, II:247

Dorset. *See* Dorsett; Daaset

Dorsett. *See also* Daaset

Dorsett, Ambjør/Ambjørg, I:202; II:102, 336

Dorsett, Anne Andresdatter, I:115

Dorsett, Edvind G., III:352–353, 366, 471

Dorsett, Even, II:102, 406–407; III:353

Dorsett, George, II:406; III:366

Dorsett, Gullik, II:102, 406, 407; III:353

Dorsett, Gullik Gulliksen, I:85–86, 99–100, 115–116, 201, 242–243, 324; II:97–98, 103, 336; III:227

Dorsett, Halvor, II:102

Dorsett, Ingeborg, II:102, 336

Dorsett, Jul/Juul/Juule Gulliksen, I:201–202, 242, 260–261, 293–294, 323–324, 367, 461–462; II:40–41, 62–63, 97, 98, 373–374, 406; III:227, 353, 366

Dorsett, Margit, II:102

Dorsett, Ole Gulliksen, I:85–86, 99–100, 115, 201–202, 242, 260–261, 324; II:98, 102–103, 336, 406–407; III:227, 352–353, 366

Dorsett, Ragnil, II:102

Dorsett, Susana Halvorsdatter, I:201–202

Doset. *See* Dorsett; Daaset

Drengerud, Anna, III:501

Drengerud, Theodore, III:410

Drivne, Steinar, III:182

Drue, Christine Carlsdatter, I:195, 196, 197, 302

Drue, Frans Ludvig/Ludwig, I:195, 196, 197, 301, 302

Durry, Carl, II:70

Dybvig/Dybvik, Harald, III:598

Dybvig/Dybvik, Karl Johan C., III:597–598

Dypdalen, Anton, III:554

Dypdalen, Ole, III:554

Dyrboeiet, Niri Hansen, I:339

Dyrebo, Gjertrud, I:214

Dyrebo, Hans Hansen, I:213–214

Døhlen, Kristoffer, II:390

Easthagen, John, III:330

Edwards, Knut, III:395, 573

Edwards, Lou, III:539

Edwards, Nels, III:395

Edwards, Ole, III:255, 256, 395

Edwards, Thor/Tor, III:395, 495, 565, 573

Eeg, Jacob Engebretsen, I:162

Eeg, Lars Johnsen, I:161, 162

Eeg, Laurine, I:161, 162, 163. *See also* Østern, Laurine Olsdatter

Eeg, Martea, I:161, 162

Eeg, Thore/Thorer Engebretsen, I:161, 162, 197, 302

Egge, Thrond S., III:484

Eggen, Erik, III:584

Eggerud, Nils Gjermundsen, I:96

Eielsen, Elling, I:66, 169, 171, 206, 207, 253, 254–255, 358, 437; II:46, 169

Eika, Halvor Klausen, II:302

Eilovsen, Ole, I:194

Einong, Aslaug Jacobsdatter, I:98

Eivindsdatter, Margit, I:200

Ekre, Ole, III:603, 604

Ekren, Andreas, III:225

Ekren, Guro, III:225, 617

Ekren, Jakob, II:209

Ekren, Oline, II:438

Elias, Lars, I:342

Eliasdatter, Hilla, I:238, 239
Ellefsen, Nils, I:268
Ellefsen, Ole, I:250, 333
Ellingsen, Elling. *See* Vold/Wold, Elling Ellingsen
Ellingsen, Ole, III:105
Ellison, O., II:263
Elmestuen, Ole Eriksen, II:351
Elnes, Johanna, III:388
Elserud. *See* Elsrud
Elsrud, Edvard Elllingsen, II:230, 285–286, 432, 433
Elsrud, Elling, I:232, 233; II:43–44, 71, 79, 99–100, 138, 146, 224–225, 253, 338
Elsrud, Elling Olsen, I:231, 233, 289, 290, 424–425, 434–435, 466; II:338; III:169. *See also* Olsen, Elling
Elsrud, Gudbrand Toresen, III:413, 428, 431
Elsrud, Gulbrand Ellingsen, II:252–253
Elsrud, Iver Ellingsen, I:424–425, 434–435, 442, 467–468; II:27, 43–44, 73, 80–81, 99–100, 139–140, 147–148, 204–205, 206–207, 224–225, 230–231, 252–253, 285–286, 338, 362–363, 432–433, 513, 514; III:169, 362, 406, 428, 431
Elsrud, Maren, I:467, 468
Elsrud, Olea Olsdatter, I:233, 290, 424–425, 434–435, 466; II:43–44, 71, 79, 99–100, 138, 146, 224–225, 338; III:169, 431
Elsrud, Ole Ellingsen, I:467, 468; II:230–231
Elsrud, Olia. *See* Elsrud, Olea Olsdatter
Elsrud, Tore, I:425

Elsrud, Tore G., II:73, 335
Elsrud, Torgrim Ellingsen, II:79, 80, 286, 334–335, 342–343, 365–366, 513–514; III:169, 285, 360, 405–406, 413–414, 427–428, 430–431, 444–445, 453, 454
Elvetun, Karen, I:185
Elvetun, Ludvig Kristiansen, I:183
Elvetun, Nils Ludvigsen, I:185
Elvttun. *See* Elvetun
Embrikson, Embrik, II:387
Embrikson, Guri, II:387
Enderson, Marta, II:143, 145, 146, 148, 149, 156, 251, 470; III:73
Enderson, Svend H., II:146, 148–149, 155–156, 197–198, 251–252, 300–301, 333, 469–470; III:73–74, 97
Endeson/Endresen/Endreson/Endson. *See* Enderson
Enge, Osuld, II:309, 425
Engebraaten, Lise. *See* Iversen, Lise
Engebretson/Engebrightson, Gaute. *See* Gunleiksrud, Gaute/Goute Ingebretsen/Engebrightson/Ingebriktson
Engeland, Christian, III:120–121
Engelhoug, Mrs., I:144
Engelstad, Jens, II:389
Engelstad, Michael, II:562; III:476
Engelstad, Nils, II:562; III:476
Engen, Jørgen, III:65, 190
Enger, Anders, III:514
Enger, Carl, III:514, 597
Enger, Fingal, II:80, 99
Engerud, Lars, I:322
Engeström, Lars von, Count, III:96
England, John, III:76

Englaugsmoen, Engebretsen, I:112
Englaugsmoen, Johan Engebretsen,
    I:94, 146
Engum, Joel Leonard, III:322,
    345, 369, 370, 371, 386, 402,
    403, 407, 437, 552
Engum, Johan, III:293, 301, 322,
    345, 370, 403, 437
Engum, John J., III:301, 322,
    368–369, 370, 402–403, 407,
    451, 483, 484, 485, 552
Engum, Mary, III:267, 293, 300–
    301, 316–317, 321–322, 345,
    370–371, 385–386, 402–403,
    407–408, 417–418, 436–437,
    451, 485–486, 552. *See also*
    Vold/Wold, Marit E.
Ensrud, Brit, II:515
Ensrud, Johan, III:102
Ensrud, John, III:102
Enstad, Ingri, II:420
Enstad, Mari, II:417, 445, 505
Enstad, Peder, II:420
Erfjord, Marta Karina
    Torkelsdatter, III:350
Erfjord, Sofie Samuelsdatter,
    III:349, 350, 359, 364, 365,
    620–621
Erfjord, Svend Svendsen, III:349–
    350, 358–359, 364–365,
    372–373, 412–413, 519–520,
    620–621
Ericksen. *See* Erickson
Erickson. *See also* Eriksen;
    Erikson
Erickson, Christen, II:359
Erickson, Martha/Marta,
    II:129–130, 282–283, 359–360,
    496–497
Erickson, Oline, II:130

Eriksdatter, Christine.
    See Dahl, Christine
Eriksdatter, Kari, I:455
Eriksen. *See also* Erickson;
    Erikson
Eriksen, Anders, II:451
Eriksen, B., I:145
Eriksen, Erik, I:65, 440; II:164,
    241, 451, 485; III:91–92, 133,
    416
Eriksen, Gunder, II:82
Eriksen, Inger, II:485; III:89, 91–
    92, 123–124. *See also* Berby,
    Inger Hansen
Eriksen, Johan Peter. *See* Lian,
    Johan Peter Eriksen
Eriksen, Mr., II:560
Eriksen, Nelly/Nælli, III:91, 92
Eriksen, Olaug Børtnes, I:440,
    441; II:53, 162–163, 164, 212,
    240, 241, 274; III:415, 416,
    442, 571, 572, 607, 608
Eriksen, Ole. *See* Sando, Ole
    Eriksen
Erikson. *See also* Erickson;
    Eriksen
Erikson, Leif, III:126
Erikson, Martha. *See* Erickson,
    Martha
Erlemoen, Jens Jørgensen, I:191,
    193, 221
Eskilsen/Eskildsen, Ole, II:471;
    III:128
Espe, Ole Olsen, I:47
Espelund, Halvor, III:175
Espeset, Henrik Selvesen, I:453
Espeset, Kari, I:453
Estanes/Ystanes, Johannes Ossden.
    See Estnes, John
Estnes, John, III:540–541, 585

Estrem, Ole Olsen, I:427, 450;
II:38, 358
Evensen, Beret, I:444
Evensen, Beret/Berit, I:444; II:220
Evensen, Elly, I:444
Evensen, Gullik. *See* Daaset,
Gullik Evensen
Evensen, Hans, I:186, 209
Evensen, Ingeborg Helgesdatter,
I:444–445; II:194, 220–221.
See also Skare, Ingeborg
Helgesdatter
Evensen, Lars, II:390, 466, 467
Evensen, Ole, I:419, 444–445;
II:194, 220–221
Evje, Ole, I:108

Fagerlien, Frans Peder, II:179
Fagerlien, Ingebrigt, II:179
Fairhair, Harald, III:375, 376
Fairhair, Ingrid, III:376
Falla/Fella, Almer, II:512, 513
Falla/Fella, Amanda, II:413
Falla/Fella, Anna, III:134, 135,
260
Falla/Fella, Carl, II:512, 513
Falla/Fella, Hilda, II:540; III:184,
185
Falla/Fella, Hilde, II:428, 429
Falla/Fella, Karen, II:467
Falla/Fella, Karl, III:134, 135, 185,
186, 260, 340, 341, 343. *See
also* Peterson, Karl
Falla/Fella, Martia/Marthea/
Martea, II:320, 378, 513
Falla/Fella, Peder/Per F., II:320,
378, 412, 429, 461, 462, 467,
513, 560, 562; III:116, 184,
185, 260
Fangen, Wilhelm, I:108

Farley/Ferlie/Ferley. *See also* Førle;
Førle/Førli
Farley/Ferlie/Ferley, Christofer,
III:471
Farley/Ferlie/Ferley, Frank, III:471
Farseth, Pauline, II:532
Fedde, Elizabeth, III:168
Fella. *See* Falla/Fella
Feragen, Alex/Axel, III:289–290,
355–356, 367–368, 521
Feragen, Emilie, III:356
Feragen family, III:516
Ferlie/Ferley. *See* Farley/Ferlie/
Ferley; Førle/Førli
Fikkan, Hellik Tostensen, I:179
Fikkan, Levor, I:339
Finhert/Finnert/Finnhert, Inger
Mikkelsdatter, II:434–435
Finhert/Finnert/Finnhert, Inger
Olsdatter, II:351, 352, 434,
441, 442, 520
Finrud/Funrud, Kittil, II:67
Finsen, Anne Dorthea, II:559
Finsen, Jakob, II:559
Fjeld, Anton, III:416
Fjeld, John/Johannes Nilsen,
I:284, 286, 335, 378–379,
421, 440, 441; II:34–35, 162,
164, 169, 211, 212, 244, 273,
440–442
Fjelde, Paul, III:584
Fjære, Alfred Hansen, III:294,
302, 306–307
Fjære, Elen Iversdatter, III:307
Fjære, Hans Nilsen, III:307
Fjære, Ingrid Arntsen, III:591
Fjære, Kasper Nilsen, III:78, 400
Fjære, Marius Nilsen, III:580,
586–587
Fjære, Nikolai Bottolfsen, III:78

Fjære, Nils Kjerskow Nilsen, III:580

Fjære, Peder Nilsen, III:307, 580

Fjærli, Jens A. Nilsen. *See* Nilsen, Jens Antonius

Fjæstad, Jens Larsen, II:60

Fjøse, Anne, I:321

Fjøse, Kittil, I:183

Flaa, Eli, III:266

Flaa, Ingeborg, III:266

Flaa, Nils, III:266

Flaa, Peder, III:266

Flaa, Trond, III:266

Flaagan, Ingeborg, II:215

Fladestøl, Christian, II:402

Fladestøl, Mikal Larsen, II:402

Fladestøl, Tønnes, I:393

Fladland, O., I:145–146

Flagestad, Kari, II:416, 418

Flagestad, Tosten Pedersen, II:415–416, 418

Flaskerud, Olav, II:224

Flata, Kjersti Helliksdatter, I:269

Flata, Ole Helliksen, I:269, 306, 326, 331

Flatbraaten, Anders, II:312

Flatbraaten, Harald, II:312

Flatbraaten, Oline, II:312

Flatbraaten, Siri, II:312

Flaten, Anders Hansen, III:518

Flaten, Gunnar, III:84

Flaten, Ingeborg, II:312

Flaten, Marie Helliksdatter, III:517–518

Flaten, Sigri, III:83, 84

Fleischer, Knud Johan, II:81

Flika, Bernt Berentsen, II:298

Flika, Pauline, II:298

Floge, Sjur, I:185

Flørenes/Flørnæs, Juliane, I:356; II:397

Folkedal, Barbara Sjursdatter, II:121

Folkedal, Mikkel Sjursen, I:174, 176–177, 219, 220

Folkedal, Svend Endresen, II:121

Folkedal, Synneve, I:174, 176–177, 220

Folkedal, Torger, II:93

Folsaas, Halvor, I:314, 315–316

Folsaas, Kitil, I:314, 315–316

Fonnli, Egil Olsen, III:494, 495, 548

Fonnli, Ole, III:494

Forbord, Marit, II:48

Fosholdt. *See* Fosholt/Fossholt

Fosholt/Fossholt, Fingal, I:425; II:43, 71–72, 73

Fosholt/Fossholt, Guri, I:425

Fosholt/Fossholt, John Torkelsen, II:334–335, 342–343, 362, 365–366; III:413–414, 427–428, 431, 444–445

Fosholt/Fossholt, Syver, I:425; II:43

Fosholt/Fossholt, Torkel Jonsen/ Johnson, II:284, 285, 312, 335; III:414

Foss, Johannes Olsen, I:145, 146, 148

Foss, Torand, I:285–286

Fossheim, Halvor. *See* Lauransson, Halvor Fossheim

Fossheim, Ole, I:83

Fossum, Hans Arnesen, I:302

Fossum, Ingeborg Johnsen, I:258

Fossum, Jacob Johnsen, I:195

Fossum, John Jacobsen, I:197

Fossum, Martine, I:301

Fossum, Ole, II:541

Fossum, Sally, III:197, 260

Fossum, Thorine, I:301

Foster, Stephen, III:92
Foyn, Miss, II:216
Foyn, Mrs., III:112–113
Foyn, Svend, II:216, 424, 426;
    III:70, 71, 112–113
Francke, August Hermann, I:255
Fredrichsen. *See also* Fredriksen
Fredrichsen, Anna Dorthea, I:357
Fredrichsen, Emil, I:358
Fredrichsen, Jacob, III:96
Fredrichsen, Mrs., I:246, 247
Fredriksdatter, Anna, III:192
Fredriksdatter, Turi, II:182
Fredriksen. *See also* Fredrichsen
Fredriksen, Fredrik Johan, III:69,
    74, 75, 79–80, 191–192
Fredsen, Fred. *See* Fredriksen,
    Fredrik J.
Frickson, Mrs., II:534
Fridrichsen, Anders Emil, I:247,
    248
Friedrichsen, Pastor. *See*
    Fredrichsen, Jacob
Frogner, Jacob/Jakob, II:233, 234
Frogner, Mother, II:232
Frogner, Nicolaus, II:293
Frovold/Frøvold, K., II:193
Frovold/Frøvold, Knut, II:193, 221
Frydendal, Mikkel, III:425
Frøines, Mathis, II:360
Frøiseth, Berendt A., I:172, 177
Fugleli, Gunder, I:437
Funrud/Finrud, Kittil, II:58
Furuholmen, Christen Rasmussen,
    III:90, 92
Furuset, Anne Pauline
    Pedersdatter, II:45, 105–106,
    110, 115–116, 158–159, 246–
    248, 259
Furuset, Beate Kristoffersdatter,
    II:248–249

Furuset, Christine Eriksdatter/
    Pedersdatter. *See* Dahl,
    Christine
Furuset, Dahl Peder Eriksen, I:426
Furuset, Erik Pedersen, II:45,
    158–159, 183–184, 201–202,
    226–227, 246, 248–249,
    258–259, 275–276, 287–288,
    348–349, 357–358, 376–377,
    465–466
Furuset, Karen. *See* Dilrud, Karen
Furuset, Kari Pedersdatter, I:427
Furuset, Pauline. *See* Furuset,
    Anne Pauline Pedersdatter
Furuset, Peder Eriksen, I:379,
    402–403, 426, 454–455; II:44–
    45, 59–60, 105–106, 110–111,
    114, 132
Furuset, Siri Kristiansdatter,
    I:402–403, 426, 454–455;
    II:44–45, 59–60, 105–106,
    110–111, 114, 132, 246,
    258–259, 275–276, 357–358
Furuseth. *See* Furuset
Førle. *See also* Farley/Ferlie/Ferley
Førle/Førli, Christopher/
    Christofer, I:115; II:98, 336,
    406
Førle/Førli, Gunnbjørg
    Helliksdatter, I:116
Førle/Førli, Hellik C., I:116, 202
Førle/Førli, Jorn, II:98
Førle/Førli, Mari, I:202
Føxebakken, Christian, I:105
Føxebakken, Ole, I:105
Føxehagen, Anders, I:104
Føxehagen, Berthe, I:104

Gaarder, Allette, II:491
Gaarder, Ole, I:450
Gaardsvoll, Kari, III:282

Gaaseberg, Christofer, II:336
Gabrielsdatter, Siri, I:342, 347
Galok, Mabel Josephine, III:130
Gamkin/Gamkind. *See* Gamkinn
Gamkinn, Hans Nielsen,
 I:351–352, 358–359, 369–370,
 373–374, 383–384
Gamkinn, Jens, I:351
Gamkinn, Niels Jensen, I:350,
 358–359, 368, 373–374,
 383–384
Gamme, Gulbrand, I:359
Garfield, James, President, II:292,
 294
Garfield, Robert, III:157
Gasmann, Hans, I:69–70, 113
Gasmann, Nella, I:68, 69, 113
Gaustad, Mathea, III:528, 549
Geving, Anne, III:64
Geving, Johan Henrik Rasmusen,
 II:375–376, 384–385, 491–492.
 See also Bjørgum, Johan
 Rasmusen
Geving, Ole Rasmussen, II:491,
 492; III:64, 110–111
Gildeskor, Tone, III:523
Gilje, Tønnes Hansen, I:296, 297
Gillund, Jens, II:276
Gjeldager/Gjeldaker/Gjeldokk,
 Botolf Botolfsen, I:447–448;
 II:137, 138
Gjeldager/Gjeldaker/Gjeldokk,
 Knut S., III:177
Gjeldager/Gjeldaker/Gjeldokk,
 Lars Nilsen, III:215, 216
Gjeldager/Gjeldaker/Gjeldokk,
 Margit, III:215–216
Gjelde, Anders, II:272
Gjerde, Christopher, I:107, 108
Gjerde, Gulbrandsen Sjulsen, I:397
Gjerde, Gullik Paulsen, I:398

Gjerde, Marit, I:437
Gjerde, Ole, I:281, 397
Gjerde, Ole H., I:281
Gjerde, Paul, I:397
Gjernes, Viking, I:176
Gjertsen, Herman, III:516
Gjertsen, Melchior Falk, II:169,
 172
Gjestrud, Tora/Thora Hansdatter,
 I:57
Gjestvang, Taale Andreas, I:86,
 91, 93, 94, 109, 112, 116, 118,
 144, 146, 147, 248
Gjømle, Anders Olsen, II:79,
 141–142, 186
Gjømle, Andres, I:201
Glesne, Even, II:91
Gløersen, Ole Kristian, II:425, 426
Godager, Adolf, I:454
Godager, Christine, I:454
Godager, Even Martinusen,
 II:276–278
Godager, Even Nilsen, II:276–278
Goderstad, Erik Olsen, III:355,
 356, 367–368, 517. *See also*
 Olson, Erick G.
Goderstad, Ole, III:290, 355, 356,
 367
Goderstad, Torje. *See* Solberg,
 Torje Olsen
Gollo, Østen Pedersen, I:218, 245
Goplerud, Levor, III:461
Goplerud, Peder, II:284
Gousdal, Fredrik Haaversen, I:347
Gousdal, Sara Haaversdatter,
 I:347
Graa, Ole, II:378
Graaterholen, Mattias, III:535
Granstuen, Hellik, I:277, 321
Granstuen, Jøran, I:235
Granstuen, Paul, I:277, 321

Gunleiksrud, Hans Ingebretsen,
I:218, 244, 245, 264; II:109–
110

Gunleiksrud, Ingebret Torstensen/
Torsteinsen, I:61–62, 123,
217–218, 244–245, 264–265,
428–429; II:109

Gunleiksrud, Kari Sigurdsdatter,
I:62, 217–218, 244–245

Gunleiksrud, Margit, I:218

Gunnes, Erik, III:266

Gunnes, Jakob, III:266

Gunnes, Kari, III:266

Gunnes, Pete, III:293

Gunnes, Ragnhild, III:264,
265–266, 275, 281

Gunnesbak, Anne, III:266

Gunnesbak, Ole, III:266

Gunness, Belle, III:436

Gunnuldsen, John, I:218

Gurine, Karen, III:578

Gustavsen, Jens, III:147–148

Guttormsdatter, Ragnild, II:331

Haabak, Knut, III:127

Haabak, Tarjei, III:127

Haaeim, Sjur Jørgensen, I:48, 52,
55. *See also* Jørgensen, Sjur

Haakenstad, Hans, III:204

Haakon VII, King, III:380

Haaltsæteren, Ole Johansen. *See*
Holtseteren/Holtsæteren, Ole
Johansen

Haanes, Bent/Bernt, I:191, 206,
222

Haarstad, Erik, III:263, 266

Haarstad, Ingebrikt, III:266

Haarstad, Karen, III:266, 291

Haatvedt/Haatveit, Nils, II:203–
204, 304

Haatvedt/Haatveit, Ole, II:203–
204

Haatvedt/Haatveit, Thor E., II:218

Haaug/Houg. *See* Haug/Houg

Haavardson, Sigbjørn, II:56

Haaversen/Haaverson, Fredrik,
II:181; III:82

Haaversen/Haaverson, Sigbjørn,
II:181, 182; III:82

Haaversen/Haaverson, Tron, I:392

Haddeland, Knut Pedersen, I:98

Haddeland, Peder Olsen, I:98

Hafdal, Halvor, III:64

Hafdal, John, III:64

Haga, Gulbrand Jensen, II:127,
129, 166, 185, 234, 293

Haga, Hans Jensen, II:127, 129,
166, 185, 234

Haga, Marie, II:166

Haga boys, II:229, 234, 332

Hage, Syver, III:172

Hagen, Anders Andersen, II:190,
219; III:88

Hagen, Andreas, III:492

Hagen, Anna, III:250

Hagen, Elling, III:128

Hagen, Emma, III:617

Hagen, Erik Eriksen, II:273

Hagen, Hans Hansen, II:488;
III:106

Hagen, Helge, II:273

Hagen, Ingeborg, III:278

Hagen, Johannes, II:190, 300, 460

Hagen, Jorgen/Jørgen, III:128, 250

Hagen, Karl, III:128

Hagen, Knut, III:225

Hagen, Syver, II:208, 310; III:225

Hagen, Tosten, II:300, 460, 487,
488

Hago, Knudt, III:68

Hago, Unn, III:108

Hald, Niels, I:356

Hall, Helge, III:361

Hallsteinsen, Hallstein, I:379, 440–441

Hallsteinsen, Olea Olsdatter, I:441

Halstensen, Rasmus, I:115

Halvorsdatter, Birgit, II:50

Halvorsen, Halvor, II:182, 402, 403; III:81

Halvorsen, Knud. *See* Dahle, Knud Halvorsen; Lehovd, Knud Halvorsen

Halvorsen, Ole C., II:288, 561; III:220, 221

Halvorsen, Paul, I:398

Halvorsgard, Ole Svensen, I:65

Hamarseie, Peder Jensen, II:259

Hammer, Hans/Jans Jakob, I:355, 358

Hammer, Helene Sophie, I:355, 358, 411; II:216

Hammer, Lars, I:358

Hammer, Lina, I:272

Hammer, Marie, I:272

Hammer, Mrs., II:39, 87, 89, 295; III:283

Hammer, Ole, III:338, 339, 348, 349, 432, 457, 466, 467

Hamre, Hellik Gulliksen, I:234

Hande, Halvar/Hallvard, III:304–305, 306

Handelsby, Martin, III:90

Hange, Hans Nielsen, I:207

Hansdatter, Mali, I:236, 239

Hansdatter, Maria/Marie, II:180

Hansebraaten, Anders Anderson Huus, III:68

Hansebraaten, Gunvor, III:68, 83

Hansen. *See also* Hanson

Hansen, A., II:186–187

Hansen, Adolf, III:139, 400

Hansen, Anton, III:355

Hansen, Conrad Martinius, III:100, 101

Hansen, Edvard/Edward, III:69, 74–75, 187, 190

Hansen, Elias. *See* Narjord, Elias Hansen

Hansen, Erik, II:73, 80, 139, 224

Hansen, Fritz, I:375

Hansen, Gine, II:376, 377

Hansen, Gulbrand, II:224–225

Hansen, H. *See* Bjokne/Bjøkne, Hans Hansen; Lehovd, Hans Hansen; Ulness/Ulsnæss, Halvor Hansen

Hansen, Hagerup, III:477

Hansen, Hansine, III:152–153

Hansen, Henrik, I:354

Hansen, Hilda, III:187, 190, 191

Hansen, Ingeborg, III:596

Hansen, Inger. *See* Berby, Inger Hansen/Hansdatter; Eriksen, Inger

Hansen, J. *See* Bjokne/Bjøkne, Jorgen/Jørgen Hansen

Hansen, Jakob/Jacob, II:371; III:152–153

Hansen, Johanne, II:512, 540–541

Hansen, John, III:134

Hansen, Kari, III:65

Hansen, M., III:185

Hansen, Miss, III:556

Hansen, Mr., III:596–597

Hansen, Mr., I:185

Hansen, Mrs., III:567, 618–619

Hansen, Niels, I:376

Hansen, Oluf, II:371

Hansen, Pastor, II:137

Hansen, Peter H., II:106, 276

Hansen, Ragnhild, III:577–578

Hansen, Samuel (S. N.), I:248, 376

Hansen, Samuel L., II:297, 454, 455, 504, 505

Hansen, Sophie, I:375

Hansen, T, II:541

Hansen, Thomine. *See* Dannevig, Thomine

Hansen family, I:354

Hanserud, Mikkel, I:460

Hanserud, Ole, I:460

Hansløkken, Sivert, III:65, 190

Hanson. *See also* Hansen

Hanson, Edvard/Edward, II:479; III:151

Hanson, Gulic, III:313–314, 490–491, 525–526, 541–542

Hanson, Hagerup, III:458

Hanson, Hans Engebretsen, II:104, 430, 431, 458, 479, 528, 543; III:188, 229

Hanson, Hilda, III:139, 140

Hanson, John/Johannes, II:311, 337–338, 393, 419; III:67

Hanson, Mrs., II:289

Hanson, Olianna, II:104, 345, 430, 431, 458, 479, 528, 538, 543, 548, 549, 553; III:65, 139, 140, 150, 151, 186–187, 188, 191, 229, 252. *See also* Olson, Olianna

Hanuk, Mrs., I:352

Harbak, Ole, III:470

Harbak, Tobias, III:470

Harrison, Ben, II:458

Harrison, Carter, Sr., III:305, 306

Harvey, Dr., III:343

Haslegard, Otto, II:456

Haslegard, Rønnaug/Rine, II:456

Haslestad, Bjørn, I:66

Hatleskog, Martha N., II:464

Hatlestad, Ole Jensen, I:215, 217

Hattrem, O. A., I:466

Haug. *See* Haug/Houg

Hauge, Gusta, I:357, 358, 375, 410, 411; II:38, 87–88, 89, 90, 216, 297, 339, 340, 347

Hauge, Hans Nielsen, I:143, 171, 207, 255, 446, 448

Hauge, Knut, III:284, 299

Haugegaarden, Ole, III:200, 235

Haugen, Anne, III:188

Haugen, Bendik, III:156–157

Haugen, C., II:419

Haugen, Godthart, III:123

Haugen, Gulbrand G., I:330; II:186

Haugen, Gunnild, III:266

Haugen, Guro Eriksdatter, II:460, 515–516

Haugen, Hans, II:219, 300, 419, 487

Haugen, Ingeborg Eriksdatter, II:300, 388–389, 460, 487

Haugen, Knut Olsen, II:388, 389, 487

Haugen, Marit Olsdatter. *See* Bjokne/Bjøkne, Marit

Haugen, Nils P., III:613, 615

Haugen, Ole, I:382, 389; II:337; III:84, 123

Haugen, Sigrid, II:219

Haugen, Simen, II:28

Haugerud, Erik Olsen, I:280, 288–289, 425, 434; II:43, 44

Haugerud, Maren Torine, I:431, 435; II:205, 206

Haugerud, Niels Julius, I:431

Haugerud, Ole, II:99, 138, 253, 338, 363, 432–433

Haugerud, Ole Hansen. *See* Rustand, Ole Hansen

Haugerud, Ole Olsen (the elder), I:231–232, 233, 259, 260, 280, 288–289, 425, 434, 435, 441–442; II:73, 80

Haugerud, Ole Olsen (the younger), I:231–232, 233, 259–260, 265–266, 267, 280, 290, 425, 441–442; II:27, 43, 44, 73, 81

Haugerud, Torgrim Olsen, I:232, 233, 259–260, 278, 425, 435, 441; II:81

Haughom, Anna, I:342

Haughom, Lars Andreas, I:393

Haughom, Peder, II:100

Haughom, Turi, II:181

Haug/Houg, Anna, III:143

Haug/Houg, Assor, III:142–143

Haug/Houg, Bertina, III:142–143

Haug/Houg, Engebret E., II:387, 447

Haug/Houg, Guri, I:420; II:32, 372, 386

Haug/Houg, Guro, I:159

Haug/Houg, Halsten/Hallsten Svendsen, I:169, 199, 420, 422–423; II:31, 33, 118–119, 327, 372, 373, 386, 387, 446, 447; III:141, 143

Haug/Houg, Helene, III:143

Haug/Houg, Ingrid, I:199, 446; I:200

Haug/Houg, Kittil/Kitil, I:447; II:31, 119, 326, 372

Haug/Houg, Knud/Knut/Knudsen/ Knutsen, I:252, 255, 285; II:31, 119, 326, 371, 373, 387, 446, 447; III:141, 142

Haug/Houg, Knud/Knut/Knudsen Larsen, I:140, 168, 169, 170, 171, 198–199, 286; II:326

Haug/Houg, Kristi, I:157

Haug/Houg, Lars Larsen, I:200, 336–337, 447; II:31, 32, 33, 326; III:143

Haug/Houg, Lars Svendsen, I:140, 169, 199, 336–337, 420, 423; II:32

Haug/Houg, Margit Halsteinsdatter, I:143; II:33, 189; III:143

Haug/Houg, Mari Larsdatter, I:142, 157, 168, 170, 171, 198, 199, 422, 447; II:32

Haug/Houg, Ole, I:448; II:31, 119; III:143

Haug/Houg, Ole Larsen, I:140, 143, 153, 157, 159, 168, 170, 198–199, 199–200, 251, 252, 283, 284, 335, 420, 446, 448; II:30, 117, 129, 188–189, 325, 327, 371, 373, 385, 446–447, 520, 521; III:140, 142

Haug/Houg, Ragnil, II:446, 521, 522

Haug/Houg, Svend/Sven Larsen, I:142–143, 153, 157–159, 171, 200, 252, 254–255, 286, 337, 422, 423, 448; II:32–33, 119, 189, 326–327, 373, 386, 387, 446–447, 521–522; III:142–143

Haug/Houg, Turid Larsdatter, II:188–189, 327, 373

Haugstvet, Dorthea, II:143, 145, 146, 148, 149; III:74

Haugstvet, Jacob/Jakob Svendesen, II:143, 145, 146, 148, 149; III:73, 74

Haukenæs, Sjur, II:121

Haukenæs, Thrond Sjursen,
II:93–94, 107–108, 120–121,
196, 480–481; III:143–144,
226, 236, 261–262, 279–280,
288–289, 320–321, 344,
410–411, 451–452, 499, 501,
504, 622–623
Haukenæs, Ulvik Thrond Sjursen.
See Haukenæs, Thrond Sjursen
Haukenæs family, III:451, 452
Haukland, Karen Anstensdatter,
I:414
Havnen, Ole Nilsen, I:185
Hebel, Udo J., II:263
Hedemark family, II:425, 454
Hedström, Oluf Gustaf, I:143–144
Hefte, Botolf, II:531; III:84
Heg, Even, I:98
Heg, Hans Christian, I:299
Heggerudstad, Iver, III:406
Heggtveit, H. G., II:499
Hegni, Tov, I:84
Heiberg, Gunnar, II:499
Helgelien, Asle K., III:436
Helgelien, Halvor K., III:434
Helgesen. *See* Lehovd; Nerdrum;
Skare
Helgaaker, Hans, I:368
Helland, Martha, III:305
Helle, Holger Petterson, I:216–217
Helleland, Johannes, III:584
Hellerud, Ole, I:319
Hellerud, Steinar Olsen, I:203
Helliksen, Mathilde Flatrud,
III:517
Helling, Margit E., III:77
Helling, Sven, I:452, 453
Helseth/Helset. *See also* Hestad
Helseth/Helset, Anders Olsen,
III:378, 379, 389, 409, 499,
567–568

Helseth/Helset, Anna, III:384
Helseth/Helset, Anne/Ane
Andersdatter, III:379, 384, 388,
567, 569
Helseth/Helset, Elias Olsen,
III:379, 380, 384, 387, 388,
408, 409, 498, 567
Helseth/Helset, Ellen Anna,
III:379, 383, 384, 388–389,
408–409, 499, 534–535, 567,
568–569
Helseth/Helset, Hans Olsen,
III:383, 384, 387
Helseth/Helset, Ingeborg
Kristiansdatter, III:534, 535
Helseth/Helset, Jens Olsen,
III:379–380, 387
Helseth/Helset, Olaf/Ole Olsen,
III:379, 384, 387, 409, 498,
567, 569
Helseth/Helset, Oline, III:383
Helseth/Helset, Peder Olsen,
III:379, 535
Hemmestveit, Mikkel, II:405
Hemmestveit, Torjus, II:405
Henderson family, I:177
Hendricks, Thomas A., II:374
Hendrickson, Anders (Andrew),
I:369, 370
Hendrickson, Ole, I:369, 370
Hendrickson family, I:453
Henningsen, Hans, III:159–160
Henningsen, Harald, III:159, 160
Henningsen, Ingeborg, III:160
Henningsen, Kristian, III:159–160
Henriksen, Elise Albertine, III:399
Henriksen, Johan, III:392–393,
399, 401
Henriksen, Ole, III:205
Henriksen, Simon Johan, III:393
Herbrandsen, Ole, I:322

Herlofsen, Axel, II:398
Hermansen, Gjert, III:355
Hersgaard, Halvor, I:64
Hersgaard, Ole, I:64
Herstad, Anton Pettersen, III:433–
  434, 467, 488–489
Hervin, Ole S., III:425
Hervin, P. S./Hverven, Peder
  Simensen, III:425
Hesjebakken, Gjermund, I:229
Hestad. *See also* Helseth/Helset
Hestad, Beret Anna, III:379, 383,
  384, 388–389, 409, 535, 567,
  569
Hestad, Elias Pedersen, III:379,
  408, 534–535, 567
Hestad, Knut Andreas, III:378,
  379, 380, 382, 384, 387, 389,
  408–409, 497, 534–535, 565,
  567, 569
Hestad, Knut Ingvald Eliassen,
  III:567
Hestad, Peder Alfred, III:499
Hestad, Siri Anna, III:388, 389,
  497, 499
Hestebrekk, Ragnhild
  Sveinsdatter, I:286
Hetager, Anton, II:542
Hetager, Ludvig, II:443, 561;
  III:114, 115, 116
Heve/Hove, Johannes, I:390
Heve/Hove, Magrete Nilsdatter,
  I:175, 176–177, 220, 240–241,
  391
Heve/Hove, Marthe, I:390–391
Heve/Hove, Ole Olsen/Olson,
  I:173, 176–177, 219, 220,
  240–241, 391, 392; II:538
Heve/Hove, Susan, I:241
Heyerdahl, Stener, I:353; II:40
Hilden, Jon, I:368

Hilton, Andor Hansen, II:369,
  371; III:81
Hilton, Anne Olsdatter, I:263,
  399, 401, 456–457; II:164, 175,
  223–224, 228, 266, 268, 288,
  291, 304–305, 331, 353, 410,
  448, 468–469, 558; III:80–81
Hilton, Annie, II:558
Hilton, August Halvorsen, II:178,
  332, 411–412
Hilton, Bertha, II:560; III:80
Hilton, Conrad, II:178, 268, 412
Hilton, Dortea/Dorthea, II:263,
  369, 371, 559
Hilton, Emily, II:450
Hilton, Gus, II:267, 332
Hilton, Hans Jakobsen, I:188, 190,
  262–263, 399, 401, 431–433,
  455, 456–457; II:127, 128,
  153, 154, 164, 175, 176, 178,
  184–185, 199–200, 223–224,
  228, 231, 234, 260, 266, 268,
  288, 289, 290, 291, 304–305,
  315, 318, 331, 352, 371, 410,
  448, 468–469, 558; III:80–81
Hilton, Iver, II:371
Hilton, Jacob Hanson/Hansen,
  I:190; II:129, 154, 166, 177–
  178, 185, 199, 200, 223–224,
  229–230, 234, 262–263, 267–
  268, 270–271, 289–290, 291,
  293, 294, 304–305, 317, 318,
  332–333, 353, 354, 369, 370,
  371, 411, 449–450, 468–469,
  559–560; III:80–81
Hilton, Jakob, I:263
Hilton, Joseph, II:558, 559
Hilton, Karen/Karin, II:263, 293,
  332, 333, 352, 353, 369, 468,
  559

Hilton, Karl, II:369, 371, 411; III:81

Hilton, Malle, II:223

Hilton, Mary, II:178, 411–412

Hilton, Oluf, I:263, 401; II:178, 223, 260, 263, 305, 318, 332, 353, 369, 370, 371, 411, 559

Hilton, Sina, II:559

Himle, Odd Johanneson, I:299

Hinden, Anne, III:188

Hjallo. *See also* Sorteberg

Hjallo, Knut, III:129–130, 132

Hjallo, Randi, III:132

Hjelle, Hans Engebretsen, II:104, 528

Hjorth, Mr., I:274

Hobson, Richard P., Lieutenant, III:228

Hoch, Carrie/Karen, II:560, 562

Hoch, Gustav, II:541

Hoff, Gunde, II:134

Hoff, Johan, II:348

Hoff, Marthe/Marthea, II:226, 227, 348

Hoff, Mikkel, II:226

Hoff, Ole Thoresen, III:177

Hoff, Per, II:276

Hoff, Torkel Torkelsen, I:287

Hofsnæs, Jeppe Svenningsen, I:186

Hofstad, Erik, II:47, 48

Hofstad, Ole, II:47, 48

Hogndalen, Knut, I:82

Hogndalen, Lavrants Knutsen, I:82

Hogndalen, Tov Lavrantsen, I:82, 84

Hol, Agnete, II:70

Hol, Anton, III:499

Holan/Holen, Lars, II:46, 208

Holberg, Ludvig, III:462–463, 465, 594

Holen, Ingeborg, III:88, 89

Holen, Johan Olsen, III:88, 89

Holen, Karoline Jonsdatter, III:88, 89

Holen, Mathias/Mattias, II:208, 310

Holen, Ole, II:208

Holen/Teigen, Kari, II:219

Holfeldt, John, I:153, 158, 190, 191

Holm, Edle, I:411

Holmen, Jens, I:55

Holmes, Mrs., II:507

Holo, Knud/Knut Larsen, II:326, 327

Holseth, Inga, III:88

Holsmarken, Helene, I:105

Holtan, Anders, II:173

Holtan, Gudbrand, I:208

Holtan, Ole Olsen, I:321

Holte, Andreas/Anders, I:357; II:309, 425–426

Holter, Christian Olausen, II:461, 462, 512

Holtseteren/Holtsæteren, Anne Nilsdatter, I:105

Holtseteren/Holtsæteren, Berthe, I:104

Holtseteren/Holtsæteren, Ingebor/Ingeborg Olsdatter, I:103, 167, 288

Holtseteren/Holtsæteren, Ole Johanson, I:105, 167, 287–288, 412–413

Holtseteren/Holtsæteren, Peder Johansen, I:103, 167, 287–288, 412–413

Homlid, Egil, I:83

Homlid, Else, I:83

Hommelia, Jul, I:437

Hopen, Hans Carlsen, III:389

Hornfeldt, Mr., I:189
Hoset, Hans, III:225
Houg. *See* Haug/Houg
Hougen, Mikkel, I:142
Hovde, Brynjolf, II:28, 29
Hovde, Sigri Larsdatter, II:50
Hove/Heve. *See* Heve/Hove
Hovengen, Christopher, I:333
Hovengen, Randi, III:272
Hoversen, Thron, I:341
Hovet, Tellef S., III:126
Hovland, Edward Syverson, III:359, 372
Hovland, Gjert, I:48
Hovland, Johannes, I:47
Hullet, Halvor Knudsen, I:386
Hunstad, Ole Olsen, I:161
Hus. *See also* Huus
Hus, Anders, III:234
Hus, Ingrid Endresdatter, II:470
Hus, Levor, I:170
Hus, Sigrid Svendsdatter, II:146
Hus, Svend/Sven Endresen/ Enderson. *See* Enderson, Svend H.
Hus, Torstein Olsen, III:418, 420
Huse, Lemek, II:247, 248
Huseby, Olaf, III:327, 328
Huset, Amund, I:440
Huset, Ane/Anne, III:272, 386
Huset, Arne, III:415
Huset, Kari Nilsdatter, I:378, 379
Huset, Lars Olsen, I:378, 379
Huset, Olaug, III:572
Huset, Ole, II:432
Husevold, Knud, I:80
Husevold, Sigrid, I:80
Husher, Ferdinand A., II:39–40, 307, 309, 347, 348, 397, 398; III:94

Husher, Theresia, II:38, 39, 309; III:94
Huslegard/Huslegarden, Otto Christiansen, II:431
Huslegard/Huslegarden, Rønnaug/ Rine, II:431; III:186, 187, 188, 190–191. *See also* Norsby/ Nørsteby/Nørstebø, Rønnaug/ Rine
Husmo, Andreas, II:177
Husmo, Malle, II:177
Hustvet, Dorthea, II:198, 470
Hustvet, Jacob Svendsen, II:198, 470
Huus. *See also* Hus
Huus, I:58
Huus, Christian Anderson, III:68
Huus, Gunvor, III:68
Hval, Engebret Olsen, I:359
Hvalen, Jon Ingebretsen, I:62
Hvamstad, Ole, I:368
Hvashovd/Hvashøvd, Anne, I:223
Hvashovd/Hvashøvd, Hellik Gundersen, I:194, 223, 224, 227, 278, 281, 282–283, 307, 319, 322
Hvashovd/Hvashøvd, Kirsti/ Kjersti Gundersdatter, I:180, 194, 214, 224, 227, 281, 322, 329. *See also* Gundersdatter, Kirsti/Kjersti
Hvashovd/Hvashøvd, Levor Torstensen, I:340
Hvashovd/Hvashøvd, Tosten Levorsen, I:106, 179, 180, 194, 208, 213, 214–215, 223, 224, 226–227, 322
Hverven, Peder Simensen/Hervin, P. S., III:425
Hvid, Hans Zahl, II:138

Hæve, Ole Olsen. *See* Heve/Hove, Ole Olsen
Høegh-Guldberg, Ove, I:69, 70, 171, 187, 199, 200, 238
Høghaug, Anders, II:99, 206
Høgkasin, Halvor, I:84
Høier, Christian, I:113
Høstteigen, Aslak Olsen, I:65
Høvolne, Ole, I:229
Høye, Barbro, III:188
Høygren, Ole, III:386
Høymyr, Ole, I:333
Høymyr, Paul, I:333

Ibsen, Sigurd, III:545, 546
Ihle, H. Jakøbsen, II:224
Ihle, Ole, II:177, 178
Ildjarnstad, Gunborg, III:607
Iljernstad, Ole, II:171
Ingebrigtson, John, I:214
Ingemoen, Gulbrand, II:283, 284
Ingvaldsen, Ingvald, III:125–126
Irgens, Mr., I:232
Iversen, Alvhild, III:303, 307
Iversen, Bertel, II:126
Iversen, Derek, I:206
Iversen, Dorthe, II:126
Iversen, Ibenhard Kristian Antonius, III:294, 302–303, 307–308
Iversen, Lars, I:240
Iversen, Lise, II:338
Iversen, Ole, I:104, 105, 167
Iversen, Peder, III:251
Iversen, Torine, II:338

Jaastad, Endre Larsen, II:264, 265
Jaastad, Inger, II:149
Jaastad, Lars, III:584
Jaastad, Ole, II:149

Jacobsen/Jakobsen. *See also* Jacobson/Jakobson
Jacobsen/Jakobsen, Abraham, I:96, 98; II:441, 442
Jacobsen/Jakobsen, Andor, II:371
Jacobsen/Jakobsen, Anna, II:109
Jacobsen/Jakobsen, Christian, III:259
Jacobsen/Jakobsen, Christopher. *See* Jacobson, Christopher
Jacobsen/Jakobsen, Guro, II:109
Jacobsen/Jakobsen, Jacob. *See* Hilton, Jacob Hanson/Hansen
Jacobsen/Jakobsen, Jacob Daniel, II:109, 110
Jacobsen/Jakobsen, John, I:161, 162
Jacobsen/Jakobsen, Karl, II:371
Jacobsen/Jakobsen, Kristofer. *See* Jacobson, Christopher
Jacobsen/Jakobsen, Lars, I:401; II:129, 185, 234, 293, 319
Jacobson, Christopher, I:188–190, 193, 262–263, 400, 401, 433, 456, 457, 458; II:129, 154–155, 165–166, 184–185, 199–200, 233, 234, 263, 268, 270, 289, 293–294, 319, 331, 332, 354, 370–371, 411, 559
Jacobson/Jakobson. *See also* Jacobsen/Jakobsen
Jacobson/Jakobson, Abraham. *See* Jacobsen/Jakobsen, Abraham
Jacobson/Jakobson, Anne Maria, II:86
Jacobson/Jakobson, Joseph, II:450
Jakobsdatter, Anne, I:401; II:129
Jakobson, Kristofer. *See* Jacobson, Christopher
Jamskar, Ole, I:100–101
Jansen. *See also* Janson

Jansen, Iver, III:604
Janson. *See also* Jansen
Janson, Drude Krog, II:426
Janson, Kristofer, II:425, 426, 474;
    III:236
Jegermoen, Gunvor, III:108, 109
Jegermoen, Syver, II:530; III:108,
    109, 199–200
Jeglum, Ragnil Knudsdatter, I:157
Jellien, Gunhild, II:553
Jellum. *See also* Jullum
Jellum, Ingeborg, I:226
Jellum, Jacob Johnsen, I:204, 225
Jellum, Johan Evensen, II:49
Jellum, Ole Evensen, II:49
Jellum, Ole Johnsen, I:226
Jensdatter, Mari, III:166
Jensdatter, Synnøve, II:163
Jensen. *See also* Jenson
Jensen, Anna, III:147–148
Jensen, Engebret, III:582
Jensen, Jens, I:88, 89
Jensen, Johan, II:287; III:325–326
Jensen, Marthe/Marte, III:529m
    550
Jensen, Nils Edward Schancke,
    I:294
Jensen family, III:479, 528
Jenson. *See also* Jensen
Jenson, Imma, I:377
Jermstad, Ole, II:495, 501
Johannesen, Hanna Jensdatter,
    III:192
Johannesen, Hans Benoi, III:192
Johansen/Johanson, Ole. *See*
    Holtseteren/Holtsæteren, Ole
    Johanson
Johansen/Johanson, Otto J., II:106
Johnsdatter, Haagine, I:258
Johnsen. *See also* Johnson
Johnsen, Leonhard, III:377, 394

Johnsen, Marius, III:310–312
Johnsen, Marthe Kristine, III:162–
    163
Johnsen, Ole, III:312
Johnsen, Peder/Pete/Pid, II:376;
    III:292
Johnsen, Serine, III:312
Johnsene. *See* Johnson
Johnson. *See also* Johnsen
Johnson, August, III:435, 436
Johnson, Hans, III:271
Johnson, Jakob B., III:139, 140
Johnson, Lars, I:299
Johnson, Larsine, III:496
Johnson, Mr., I:87
Johnson, Ole, III:139, 140
Johnson, Othelius, III:135–136
Johnsrud. *See also* Jonsrud
Johnsrud, Jens, III:454
Jonassen, Jonas Albin, III:303
Jondalen, Sjul, I:396
Jonsdatter, Olava, I:191
Jonsen, Johan. *See* Bleka, Johan
    Jonsen
Jonsen, Turid, III:132
Jonsrud. *See also* Johnsrud
Jonsrud, Gulbrand, I:280; II:140
Jonsrud, Gunvald, II:140
Jon the Fiddler, I:229
Joramo, Hans Andresen, III:242
Jordet, Marit, III:286
Jordet, Ragnhild, III:242
Jordet, Syver S., III:212, 213, 241
Josiasdatter, Johanna, II:376
Jullum. *See also* Jellum
Jullum, Iver, III:64
Justen, Andeas, III:67
Justen, Guro, III:67. *See also*
    Bjokne/Bjøkne, Guri/Guro
    Johannesdatter
Juveli/Juvelie, Kjersti, I:269

Juveli/Juvelie, Knut Klemetson/
    Klemmetsen/Klemetsrud, I:249,
    250, 269; II:98
Juveli/Juvelie, Ole, II:98
Jødestøl, Bergitte, II:298
Jødestøl, Bernt Vermudsen, II:298
Jødestøl, Gabriel Gabrielsen,
    I:347, 393, 394, 406; II:56;
    III:82, 193
Jødestøl, Haavard/Haaver, II:56,
    181, 182
Jødestøl, Nils Andreas, II:555
Jødestøl, Peder Christian, I:347–
    348
Jødestøl, Siri, I:347, 394; III:193
Jødestøl, Turi, II:182
Jøranbyhaugen, Knut, I:229
Jørandby, Marit, I:229
Jørandby, Ole, II:558
Jørgensen, Arne. *See* Brager, Arne
    Jørgensen
Jørgensen, Sjur, I:50, 58. *See also*
    Haaeim, Sjur Jørgensen

Kaarfeld, Ole, I:287
Kaasa, Ole Gunleiksen, I:97
Kaasalien, Hans, II:530; III:77,
    108
Kalbakken, Hans, III:492
Kalbakken, Jacob, III:597
Kalbakken, Kristine, III:492, 510
Kalderud, Syver/Syvert, I:382, 389
Kalvehaven/Kalvehagen, Peder,
    II:309, 425
Kampestad, Ambjørg, I:386
Kampestad, Kittil, I:235
Kantum, Andreas, II:273
Kantum, Halsten Halstensen,
    II:284
Karlsen, Konrad, III:299
Karlsrud, Anfinn, I:80

Karlsrud, Gro Anfinnsdatter, I:80,
    82
Karlsrud, Hans, I:80
Karlsrud, Ole Stensen, I:81–82,
    228
Karlsrud, Sigrid, I:80
Karlsrud, Sten Olsen, I:80, 82
Karlsrud, Søren, I:80, 82
Karlstad, Martha, II:276
Kasberg. *See also* Casberg
Kasberg, Alex, III:466–467
Kasberg, Anna, III:466–467
Kasberg/Casberg, Laura. *See*
    Solberg, Laura
Kelley. *See also* Killi/Killy
Kelley, Monroe, III:287
Kellogg, John Harvey, III:489
Kelly. *See* Killi/Killy
Killi/Killy, E., III:172
Killi/Killy, Erland Rolfsen, III:173
Killi/Killy, Hans P., III:287, 551,
    604
Killi/Killy, Marie/Maria J., II:180;
    III:172–173, 212–213, 242–243,
    286–287, 455–456, 550–551,
    604
Killi/Killy, Ole Eriksen, III:171,
    173
Killi/Killy, Paul/Paal S., I:466;
    II:180; III:173, 213, 604
Killi/Killy, Ragnhild, III:242
Killi/Killy, Simen, III:170, 172,
    173
Killi/Killy, Syvert/Sever/Syver,
    I:404, 417; III:286, 287, 551,
    604
Killi/Killy, Tosten, III:173
Kinsarvik, Helge, II:405

Kinsarvik, Lars Trondsen, II:265;
III:304, 306, 327–328, 352,
420, 446, 544, 545–546,
583–584, 592
Kinsarvik, Ole, III:306
Kjelshus, Erlend/Erland Olsen,
II:191, 192
Kjensrud, Erik, II:284, 312, 463;
III:461
Kjensrud, Gunder, III:531
Kjensrud, Ole, II:284, 312, 463;
III:461
Kjenstad, Sjønne, II:535
Kjos, Nils, I:104
Kjærland, Knut, II:93
Kjølset, Knut Gulliksen, I:116
Kjølseteie, Ole, I:322
Kjølvig, Nils, III:359
Kjølvig, Ove Torgersen, II:276
Kjønstad, Christian, II:467, 561
Kjønstad, Ida, II:512
Kjønstad, Johanne, III:196
Kjønstad, Maria/Marie, III:114,
115, 116, 133
Kjønstad, Mina, II:442, 490, 512.
See also Solem, Mina
Kjønstad, Sjønne, III:134, 196,
249
Kjørsvik, Jakob Ericksen, III:388
Klemetsrud. *See also* Klemmetsrud
Klemetsrud, Herman H., I:229
Klemetsrud, Knut. *See* Juveli/
Juvelie, Knut Klemetson/
Klemmetsen/Klemetsrud
Klemmetsrud. *See also* Klemetsrud
Klemmetsrud, Anna, II:163
Klemmetsrud, Arne, III:607
Klemmetsrud, Erik, II:558;
III:376, 461
Klemmetsrud, Halsten/Halstein,
III:376, 607

Klemmetsrud, Herman, II:556
Klemmetsrud, Kristofer, II:284,
312
Klemmetsrud, Marit
Hermansdatter, II:53, 163, 240,
241. *See also* Lee, Marit
Klemmetsrud, Ole, III:376, 607
Klemmetsrud, Syver Hermansen,
III:230
Klemmetsrud boys, II:284–285
Klev, Steinar, II:49
Kleve, Knut, I:321; II:331
Kleven, Gilbert, II:331
Kleven, Iver, II:328, 331
Kleven, Pastor, II:282
Kleven, Paul Paulsen, II:41
Klungsøyr, Jakob, II:125
Klyvset, Lars, III:177
Knud/Knut/Knudsen/Knutsen,
II:31, 119, 326, 371, 373, 387,
446, 447
Knudsen. *See also* Canuteson;
Knudtson; Knutsen
Knudsen, Aanon, I:146
Knudsen, Arne, I:300
Knudsen, Bent, I:186
Knudsen, Bergitte, II:504, 505
Knudsen, Halvor, I:186, 209
Knudsen, John, II:505
Knudsen, Knud, I:54, 55, 146
Knudsen, Ole. *See* Canuteson, Ole
Knudsen, Svend. *See* Lothe/Lote,
Svein Knudsen
Knudsen, Tallak, I:55, 145
Knudtson. *See also* Canuteson;
Knudsen; Knutsen
Knudtson, Anne, III:536
Knudtson, Bergit, III:271, 426,
429, 452–453, 536, 540
Knudtson, Gunhild, III:536

Knudtson, Ole, III:428–429, 452–453, 536, 540

Knudtson family, III:426

Knutsen. *See also* Canuteson; Knudsen; Knudtson

Knutsen, Knut. *See* Haug/Houg, Knud/Knut Knudsen/Knutsen

Knutsen, Lavrants. *See* Hogndalen, Lavrants Knutsen

Knutsen, Nils. *See* Gudmundsrud, Nils Knutsen

Kodalen, Sjur, II:82

Kolberg, Captain, III:472

Kolgrav, Hendrik, II:360

Kolhus, Halstein, III:606

Kolkinn, Guri, II:58, 79

Kolkinn, Hellik, II:57, 58–59, 68

Kolkinn, Jøran, II:68, 78

Kolkinn, Niri Gudbrandsen, II:42, 79, 87, 141

Kolkinn, Ole, II:57, 86, 187, 242

Koller, Ole, I:359

Kolsgaard, Torstein Olsen, III:612

Kolstad, Mrs., II:38, 39

Kongsvold, Anne, III:242, 243

Kongsvold, T., III:241, 243

Konow, Wollert, III:558

Konstadli, Syverine, II:555

Konstadli, Syvert, II:555

Konstali, Ingebor Sofie Mortensdatter, I:393

Konstali, Severine, I:405–406

Konstali, Sigbjørn, I:393

Konstali, Syverine Toresdatter, II:113

Konstali, Trond, I:393

Koppang, Ole, I:214

Koppangen, Jul Torgersen, I:269

Koren, Elisabeth, I:411, 412; III:507

Koren, Nils, III:506

Koren, Ulrik Vilhelm, I:292; II:358; III:116, 506, 507

Kornitzer, Emily, II:450

Kornkveen/Kornkven, Kristen Guttormsen, II:310, 388, 515, 516

Korsvold, Erik, III:603

Korum, Johan, III:90

Kosberg, Peder, III:386

Kovehagen, Tarjei, III:126

Kramvik, Ole, III:237

Kristensdatter, Ane (Dala Granny), I:236, 239

Kristensen. *See also* Christensen

Kristensen, Kristian, III:400

Kristensen, Miss, II:277

Kristiansen. *See also* Christiansen

Kristiansen, Anna Elisabeth/ Elizabet, III:303, 399

Kristiansen, Gerhard, III:294, 302–303, 306, 307, 308, 392–393, 399, 400, 401, 458, 477, 537, 559–560, 577–578, 580, 586–587, 591–592

Kristiansen, Guttorm, III:109

Kristiansen, Margrete, III:109

Kristoffersdatter, Maria, II:320, 321, 356, 379–380, 443–444, 466

Kristoffersdatter, Mathea, II:562

Kristoffersen, Ole, II:412, 413

Krog, C. Ove/Ove C., I:98

Kroka, Svein Aanondsen, III:126

Krokan, Halvor Abrahamsen, I:96

Krokan, Mattis Helleksen, I:97

Krosshus, Mathis Mathiassen, I:66

Krostu, Gunsten Gunstensen, II:441, 442

Kruggerud, Ole, I:368

Kulpen, Hans Pedersen, I:359

Kvam, Eli O., II:392

Kvam, Olivia, III:388
Kvammen, S., III:105
Kvandal, Lars, II:93
Kvernbraaten, Guri, II:73
Kvernes, Christen, III:290
Kvernes, Halvor, III:290, 367
Kvia, Tobias Tørresen, I:295
Kvilekval, John, I:175
Kvinen, Ragnild Nilsdatter, I:175
Kyn, Christian Ulrik, I:165
Kølle, Catharine Hermine, I:54, 55
Kølle, Misses, I:55

Laaming, Amund, II:145
Laiem, Niels Olsen, I:219
Lambrecht, Mr., II:38
Lampland, Hellik, III:518
Lampland, Helmine, III:518
Lampland, Marie, III:517–518
Lande, Anders, I:208, 213
Lande, Anne Andersdatter, I:381, 387; II:78, 87, 241, 363–364
Lande, Christopher, III:353
Lande, Gullik Andersen, I:329, 381; II:68
Lande, Hellek Gulbrandsen/ Gulbrandson/Gulbranson. *See* Branson, Hellek G.
Lande, Kari, I:213, 381
Lande, Ole Andersen, I:234
Lande, Ole Gulbrandsen, I:381, 387, 389; II:41–42, 57, 59, 67–68, 78–79, 86–87, 141–142, 187–188, 241, 243, 363–364, 433
Lande, Ole Toresen, II:67–68, 78–79
Landeiet, Ole Helliksen, I:227
Landerud, Kristoffer, II:373
Landon, Hazel, III:526

Landstad, M. B., III:145
Lang, Tron, I:191, 206
Langaard, Conrad, I:412; III:70, 71–72, 94
Langaard, Mads, I:412
Langaard, Niels, I:412
Langbak, Ole, III:386
Langdalen, Hans, I:463, 465; II:28
Langdalen, Ole, I:463
Langeid, Eivind Taraldsen, III:126
Langeland, Knud, I:177
Langrud, Tofte, II:86
Laque, Brynnild. *See* Lekve, Brynjulv
Larsdatter, Guri, II:387
Larsdatter, Sigrid, III:131
Larsen, Anna, III:266
Larsen, Anne Eriksdatter, II:234
Larsen, Birgit Opsata, I:362
Larsen, Christian M., II:403
Larsen, Esten, I:191, 205, 221, 239
Larsen, Ingeborg, II:395–396, 550, 551
Larsen, Iver, I:241
Larsen, Jacob/Jakob, I:401; II:234
Larsen, John, I:186
Larsen, Julius, II:367
Larsen, Lars, I:337, 448
Larsen, Laur, II:76, 77
Larsen, Martin, III:467
Larsen, Mr., II:562
Larsen, Ola, I:362
Larsen, Ole, I:401; II:129. *See* Haug, Ole Larsen
Larsen, Paul, II:188–189, 395, 396
Larsen, Peder, III:266
Larsen, Sigbjørn, III:598
Larsen, Sofie Tonette, III:597–598
Larsen, Svend. *See* Haug, Svend/ Sven Larsen
Larsgaarden, Birgit, III:181

Larsgaarden, Erik, III:141
Larsgaarden, Kari, II:530
Larsgaarden/Larsgard, Ola/Ole,
  III:109, 144, 198
Larson. *See* Larsen
Lathus, Erik Nilsen, I:161, 162
Laufersweiler, Mary, II:178,
  411–412
Lauransson, Gunhild, I:83, 84
Lauransson, Halvor Fossheim,
  I:83, 84
Lauransson, Ingeborg, I:83, 84
Lauransson, Jorand Halvorsdatter,
  I:83, 84
Lauransson, Ole, I:84
Lauransson, Tov, I:84
Laverace, Ole. *See* Lauransson,
  Ole
Lawrence, Ernest O., I:84
Lawrence, Ole. *See* Lauransson,
  Ole
Lee, Robert E., General, I:340
Lee/Lie. *See also* Li; Lian/Lien;
  Snekkerlia/Snekkerlien
Lee/Lie, A., I:434
Lee/Lie, Albert, II:415; III:562
Lee/Lie, Anders Andersen, II:162–
  163, 172, 241, 254, 271, 274,
  283, 311, 328, 380, 414–415,
  434, 440, 442, 462, 483–484,
  517, 519, 520, 544, 556; III:117,
  206, 230, 233, 245, 277, 330,
  375–376, 380, 415–416, 440,
  443, 459, 501, 530–531, 560,
  570, 572, 605, 608
Lee/Lie, Anders/Andrew/Andreas/
  Andrias, I:299; II:53, 459,
  487, 489–490, 495, 501–502,
  526–527, 537, 538, 543, 544,
  548–549, 553, 554; III:64–65,
  75–76, 128, 139, 140, 151, 174,
  187, 188, 190–191, 214–215,
  228, 250. *See also* Lian,
  Anders/Andrew Johansen
Lee/Lie, Anders Nilson, I:299
Lee/Lie, Anders Olsen, I:228,
  308–309, 377, 438, 458;
  II:52–53, 116–117, 157–158,
  160, 169, 210, 235, 241, 243,
  254, 271, 283, 311, 328, 350,
  351, 380, 414–415, 433, 435,
  438, 440, 442, 462, 483–484,
  517, 544, 556; III:117, 612. *See
  also* Snekkerlia, Andreas Olsen
Lee/Lie, Anna, II:538, 543, 544,
  548, 549, 553–554; III:64,
  65, 139–140, 150–151, 190,
  251–252
Lee/Lie, Anne. *See* Snekkerlien,
  Anne
Lee/Lie, Aslak, I:229, 230; I:308
Lee/Lie, Beret/Berit, II:257, 314,
  557; III:121, 246, 336, 572
Lee/Lie, Eli Jonsdatter, I:97
Lee/Lie, Gunnild Haraldsdatter.
  See Belgum, Gunhild/Gunnild
Lee/Lie, Guttorm Olsen, I:299,
  308–309, 377–378, 379,
  440–441; II:52, 53, 116–117,
  157–158, 160, 162, 163, 170,
  172, 210, 211, 212, 213, 240,
  241, 243–244, 257, 314, 328;
  III:120, 121, 336, 337, 571, 572
Lee/Lie, Halsten/Halstein, II:284;
  III:607
Lee/Lie, Inger, II:434, 442, 520
Lee/Lie, Ingrid, II:546

Lee/Lie, Iver Andersen, II:171, 241, 245, 257–258, 274, 284, 285, 314, 335, 351, 464, 483–484, 520, 546; III:121, 209, 248, 279, 382, 444, 461, 504, 563, 611–612

Lee/Lie, Jenny, III:271

Lee/Lie, Jonas, II:308, 309, 426

Lee/Lie, Karen, II:517; III:209, 504, 612

Lee/Lie, Kari Mikkelsdatter, II:160, 169, 172, 210, 211, 235, 243, 254, 271, 283, 311, 328, 351, 380, 544

Lee/Lie, Knud, I:308

Lee/Lie, Mari Olsdatter, II:116–117, 157–158

Lee/Lie, Marit, I:229, 230; II:163, 164; II:284. *See also* Klemmetsrud, Marit Hermansdatter

Lee/Lie, Mikkel/Mekkel Andersen, II:53, 258, 274, 285, 314, 328, 330, 350, 351, 382, 414–415, 441–442, 545–546, 558; III:117, 120, 121, 209, 232–233, 247–248, 278, 335, 375–376, 415–416, 442, 444, 461–462, 464–465, 530–531, 562, 572, 607–608, 611, 612

Lee/Lie, Mikkel/Mekkel H., III:607

Lee/Lie, Ole Andersen, II:163–164, 171–172, 213, 235, 245, 254–255, 257, 258, 271, 272–274, 285, 331, 382, 383, 415, 520, 545; III:121–122, 336–337, 612

Lee/Lie, Ole Jørgensen/Jorgensen, II:537–538, 549

Lee/Lie, Ole Olsen/Olson, I:309, 378–379, 440, 460; II:52–53, 157, 158, 170, 458–459, 477, 479, 528, 538, 543, 543, 544, 549, 554, 558; III:251, 376, 464

Lee/Lie, Ole T., III:246

Lee/Lie, Ragnild Guttormsdatter, II:311

Lee/Lie, Siri Mikkelsdatter, II:160, 163, 171, 172, 211, 240; III:121, 531

Lee/Lie, Torgrim Olsen, I:229–230, 308; II:163, 164, 210–211, 241; III:121

Leerfald/Lerfald, Alma Mathilde, II:279

Leerfald/Lerfald, Hans Petter, II:279, 295

Leerfald/Lerfald, John Olsen, II:249–250, 279, 294–295

Leerfald/Lerfald, Karl Ludvig Olsen, II:249–250, 279, 294–295

Leerfald/Lerfald, Ole Olsen, II:250

Leerfald/Lerfald, Theodore, II:249–250, 279

Lehovd, Bereta/Berthea/Bertha, I:436; II:341; III:85

Lehovd, Hans Hansen, III:314

Lehovd, Helen Severine, II:341; III:85

Lehovd, Hellik/Helleik Olson/ Olsen, I:178, 179–180, 182, 183, 193–194, 207–208, 214, 223–224, 228, 234–235, 249–250, 270, 278, 283, 306–307, 321, 329, 330–331, 332, 334, 338–339, 339–340, 364–365, 387, 394, 398, 438; II:150–151, 167–168, 173, 340–341; III:85–86, 429

Lehovd, Henry Olaus, I:364; II:341; III:85

Lehovd, Ingebjørg Gulliksdatter, III:314

Lehovd, Joran/Jøran/Jorand/Jørand/Julia Halvorsdatter Gjerdeeie, I:84, 235, 339, 340, 366, 387, 397–398, 438; II:173

Lehovd, Joran/Jøran/Jorand/Jørand/Julia Paulsdatter, I:182, 193–194, 213, 223–224, 226, 235, 306–307, 319, 326, 330, 334, 338, 339, 363, 384, 395, 398, 436; II:150, 151, 173

Lehovd, Julia/Joran Olina, I:326, 364, 365, 385; II:150, 167, 172, 341; III:85

Lehovd, Knud, I:339, 340, 436, 437, 438

Lehovd, Knud Halvorsen, I:366, 387, 396, 397, 398

Lehovd, Knut Olsen, I:235; II:150–151, 167–168, 341; III:86

Lehovd, Lovisa, II:341; III:85

Lehovd, Ole Helgesen, I:108, 177, 193–194, 207–208, 213, 223–224, 226, 234–235, 249–250, 267, 270, 276, 278, 306–307, 319, 326, 330, 338, 339, 340, 363, 365, 384, 394, 397, 436; II:150–151, 167–168

Lehovd, Ole Olsen/Olson, I:182, 183, 214, 235, 268, 281, 283, 307, 322–323, 326, 327, 334, 338–339, 364, 366, 386, 387, 397, 398, 436, 437; II:117, 151, 167, 172–173, 341; III:429

Lehovd, Paul Olson/Olsen, I:235, 339, 340, 364, 365, 366, 386, 387, 394, 395–396, 398, 437; II:150, 151, 167–168, 173, 341; III:85

Lehovd, Sjul, I:398

Lehovd, Syvert, I:385

Lehovdeie/Lehovdeiet, Sjul Hansen, I:364, 386

Lei, Andreas. *See* Lee/Lie, Anders/Andrew/Andreas/Andrias

Leikvold, Ole Syversen, I:65

Lekve, Arne Brynjulvsen, I:49

Lekve, Brynjulv, I:54–55

Lekve, Herborg, I:55

Lekve, Sjur, I:55

Leqve, B. *See* Lekve, Brynjulv

Lerberg, Thorvald/Torvald Haansen, II:512, 541

Lerche, Vincent Stoltenberg, II:309

Leren, Peter/Peder/Petter D., III:63–64

Leren, Tommas, II:47, 48

Lerfald. *See* Leerfald/Lerfald

Lessing, Gotthold Ephraim, III:93, 96

Letmolia, Levor H., I:328

Leversen/Levorsen, Thostein/Tosten. *See* Hvashovd/Hvashøvd, Tosten Levorsen

Li. *See also* Lee/Lie

Li, Ingeborg, III:282

Li, Lars, III:282

Li, Tor, III:603

Lia, Erik, II:43, 558; III:376, 607

Lia, Karen, I:230

Lia, Ole Olson/Olsen, I:223, 396, 437

Liane, Hans, I:58

Liane, Knud Ellingsen, I:58

Lian/Lien. *See also* Lee/Lie

Lian/Lien, Anders/Andrew Johansen, II:486–487, 489–490, 495, 501–502, 527. *See also* Lee/Lie, Anders/Andrew/Andreas/Andrias

Lian/Lien, Anne, I:229

Lian/Lien, Erik Thorsteenson/Torstenson, I:151, 152

Lian/Lien, Guri, III:177

Lian/Lien, Ingeborganna/Ingborganna Andersdatter, II:391, 489–490, 493, 501–502, 554; III:174, 214–215, 228, 250

Lian/Lien, Jakob Johansen, II:489–490, 493, 501–502, 526–527; III:75–76, 128, 214–215

Lian/Lien, Johannes, I:222

Lian/Lien, Johan Peter Eriksen, II:471–472, 489–490, 493, 501–502, 554; III:174, 214–215, 228, 250

Lian/Lien, Kari A., III:386

Lian/Lien, Levor/Levord, I:229, 230

Lian/Lien, Nup, I:467

Lian/Lien, Sigri Iversen, III:190

Lie, Andrei/Endru. *See* Lee, Anders/Andrew/Andreas/Andrias

Lie/Lii. *See* Lee/Lie; Lian/Lien; Snekkerlien

Lien. *See* Lian/Lien

Lillebjøkne, Anne H., III:617

Lillebjøkne, Hans J., III:617

Lillebjøkne, Matias/Mathias H., III:225, 617

Lillehaugen, Knut, III:129

Lillehaugen, Sigri/Sigrid, III:83–84, 97, 129, 177, 179

Lillehaugen/Lillehaug, Tosten Mikkelsen, III:129, 131

Lillejordet, Trond, II:310

Lincoln, Abraham, President, I:304, 306, 328, 331, 337; II:341; III:509

Lind, Hans Nilsen, II:423, 475–476; III:194–195

Lind, Nils Hansen, II:408–409, 422, 475, 476

Lind, Ole Hansen, II:408–409, 475, 476

Lindaas, Anders, I:183

Lindaas, Ole, II:173

Lindberg family, I:90, 93

Lindblom, Mr., I:127–128, 131, 132

Lindboe, Ole, I:321, 323

Lindeland, Anne, II:280

Lindeland, Osmund, II:92

Lindeland, Tore, II:113

Lindelien, Lars Olsen, I:266, 280, 289

Lindeman, Ludvig M., II:123

Lindeman, Ole Andreas, II:123

Linderot/Linderoth, Lars, I:187, 292, 397

Linken, President. *See* Lincoln, Abraham, President

Linsø, Erland, I:404

Lirhus, Anders Nilson, I:299

Lisbraaten, Mikkel, II:558; III:376

Lisbraaten, Randi, II:163

Lise, Inger, II:548

Listøl, Odmund, I:393

Listøl, Sigbjørn, I:393

Liubraaten, Hans Nilsen, II:407

Liubraaten, Helge Kristiansdatter, II:407

Liubraaten, Sevat. *See* Vik, Sevat Olsen

Løne, Haldor Brynjulfsen, I:172, 173, 177
Løvaas, Karen Aamotstuen, II:467; III:134, 135
Løvaas, Theodore, II:390; III:134, 135
Løvenskiold family, I:165
Løvodden, Sigvald, I:84
Løvvold, Hans, III:559–560

Maatterud, Henrik, II:219
Magnus, Morten Henrik, III:70, 461, 465
Malchus, III:464, 465
Mark. See Mærk/Mark
Markusen, Peter, II:89
Marskal, Mr., I:135
Marum, Johannes Olsen, II:109
Mathews, Thomas Miller, I:358
Matthews, Emma, I:273, 358, 411
McCumber, Senator, III:614
McKinley, William, President, III:122, 174, 176, 228, 261, 289
Medaas, Lars Iversen, I:240, 241
Medalen, Amund Helgesen, II:82, 90, 91
Medgaarden, Knut, I:453
Medgaarden, Ole, I:453
Medgaarden, Tollef, I:453
Megaard, Hans, III:526
Megaarden, Turi T., II:137
Meidel, Lars, I:156, 159
Meidell, Ditmar, I:323
Meier, Elling, I:425
Meier, Paul, I:425
Melanchthon, Philip, III:416
Melbostad, Gulbrand, I:351
Melbostad, Maria Olsdatter, I:351, 359, 368, 370
Melby, Ole, II:380, 467
Melbye, Lars, II:390

Meldahl, Emil, II:90
Meldahl, Ferdinand, III:93, 96
Meldahl, Tony, II:90
Meldahl, Torg, III:93
Melgaard, Engebret, III:416
Melha, Emma, II:561
Meling, Pastor, II:182
Mellom, Hilda, III:184, 185
Mellom, Ole I., II:534, 540; III:184
Mesunt, Ole Christensen, II:42, 87
Michelsen, Ragnhild, III:614
Mickalson/Mickelsen. See also Mikkelsen
Mickalson/Mickelsen, Gea Marie, II:130
Mickalson/Mickelsen, Haavard/ Haaver, II:130, 283, 496, 497
Midnes, Lars, III:296
Midtboe, Johanne Maria Petersdatter, II:65, 66
Midtboe, Peter, II:66
Midtfjeldsaa/Midfelse, Anne, I:348, 394
Midtfjeldsaa/Midfelse, Sivert, I:348, 393, 394
Midtfjeldsaa/Midfelse, Syverine, II:195
Midtfjell/Midtfjells, Ole Tobias, II:75, 92, 113, 195, 356
Midtun, Lars J., II:283
Midtun, Margrete, II:497
Miesegaes, Did., I:92
Mikkelsen. See also Mickalson/ Mickelsen
Mikkelsen, Håvard, III:204
Mikkelsen, Iver, II:245
Mikkelsen, Mikkel, III:422
Miller, Mr., III:164
Misten, Andor Jakobsen, III:458, 477

Mo, Lars Olsen, I:209
Moan, Elling, II:471; III:128
Moe, Oluf, III:474, 529–530
Moen/Møen, Eli Helgesdatter,
    I:443; II:194, 307
Moen/Møen, Elise Ionette, II:193
Moen/Møen, Gulbrand O., III:120
Moen/Møen, Gunder Johnsen/
    Johnson, I:319, 419, 443, 445;
    II:49, 82, 90–91, 193–194, 307
Moen/Møen, Ingeborg, II:535
Moen/Møen, Jens, III:454
Moen/Møen, John, I:419
Moen/Møen, Lars Johannesson,
    I:299
Moen/Møen, Marit, III:272
Moen/Møen, Ole, I:440; II:312,
    366, 441
Moen/Møen, Siri, I:229
Molden, Ole, II:279
Moller/Møller, Fredrik Andreas,
    II:97
Moller/Møller, F. W., II:96
Moller/Møller, Hans E., I:56
Moller/Møller, Mrs., I:411, 412
Moller/Møller, Niels, I:410; II:89
Moller/Møller, Ole, II:284
Moller/Møller, Rennild, I:410, 450
Moller/Møller family, I:352
Monen, Elen, I:355
Monsen, Ole, II:225
Monsen, Trond, III:360
Mork, Johannes, I:155
Mork, Kirsti Jakobsdatter Søndre,
    I:200
Mortensen, Peder. See Nordhus,
    Peder Mortensen
Motterud, Jørgen, III:225
Munch, Andreas, III:331, 337
Myli, Levor Herbrandsen/
    Hærbrandsen, I:64, 65, 66

Müller, Anne, I:450
Müller, Mrs., I:375
Myran/Myrand, Anders, II:214
Myran/Myrand, Andres, I:430
Myran/Myrand, Eli, I:310, 430
Myran/Myrand, Gunder, I:430;
    II:214, 215
Myran/Myrand, Helge Nilsen/
    Nelson, I:429, 430, 431; II:214,
    215
Myran/Myrand, Ingrid
    Helgesdatter, I:290, 310, 431;
    II:214–215, 306
Myran/Myrand, Ole Aslesen,
    I:291, 292, 306, 310–311, 314–
    315, 429–430, 431; II:214–215,
    306
Myrben/Myrbøen, Anund Olsen,
    II:523; III:397, 482–483, 494,
    495, 548
Myrben/Myrbøen, Egil, III:396,
    397, 547
Myrben/Myrbøen, Margit, II:523
Myrben/Myrbøen, Ole Olsen,
    III:239, 396, 397, 483, 494,
    495, 547, 548, 565, 573, 579
Myrbøen. See Myrben/Myrbøen
Myren, Ingeborg Anna, III:388
Myren, Kari, III:272
Myro, Tor. See Ulshagen, Thor/
    Tor Torsen
Myrseth, Anders Andersen,
    III:308, 312
Mærk/Mark, Arnt, Johnsen,
    III:273, 274
Møen. See Moen/Møen
Møglestue, Bina, II:89
Møglestue, Karen/Kaja. See
    Poppe, Karen/Kaja

Naas, Mrs., III:163

Naess/Næss, Ansteen Johnsen, I:125, 139

Naess/Næss, John, I:139

Naess/Næss, Kari, III:425

Naess/Næss, Olaus, II:442

Narjord, Ane Kristine Tørrisdatter, I:193, 222, 239

Narjord, Elias Hansen, I:192–193, 207, 222, 239

Narjord, Hans Pedersen, I:190, 204, 220, 236, 239

Narjord, Peder, I:239

Narum, Iver Olsen, I:154, 158

Narverud, Ole Andersen, I:66–67, 108

Narvesdatter, Gullaug, I:152

Nattestad/Nasta, Ansten, I:123

Nattestad/Nasta, Ole Knudsen, I:120, 122, 123

Nattestadvangen. *See* Nøttestadvangen

Nederum. *See also* Skare

Nedland, Anne Berte Tallaksdatter, I:347–348

Nedland, Bertine, III:254

Nedland, Lars Andreas, III:254

Nedrebraaten, Knut, III:129, 180

Nelp, Kristine Olsdatter, II:379, 380, 390, 412, 413, 541

Nelsen/Nelson, Thom, II:241–242, 243

Nelson. *See also* Nilsen

Nelson, Christine, II:259

Nelson, David T., III:507

Nelson, Even, III:222

Nelson, Helge, I:430

Nelson, Jacob, II:201

Nelson, John, III:469–470, 564

Nelson, Knute, II:510; III:143–144, 174, 226, 236, 261–262, 279–280, 288–289, 320–321, 344, 451–452, 613, 614

Nelson, Knut L., III:180

Nelson, Nels Jacob, II:134

Nelson, Nils, III:222

Nelson, N. K., III:580

Nelson, Olaf, II:532; III:60, 137–138, 144–145, 146, 175–176, 182–183, 200, 201, 203, 206, 215, 216, 218–219, 222, 223, 233

Nelson, Syverine, II:376, 377

Nelson/Nelsen, Thom, II:241–242, 243

Nerby, Ole, III:376

Nerdrum, Fingar/Fingal Helgesen, II:81–82, 91, 194

Nerdrum, Helge Gundersen. *See* Skare, Helge Gundersen

Nerland, Ole Olsen, III:470

Nerlie, Anders, I:395, 397–398

Nerlie, Joran, I:398

Nes, Johanne, I:209

Nes, Ole, I:212

Nesberg, Ole Olsen, I:296, 297

Neset, Jon/John Jonsen, II:523, 539, 540; III:397, 483, 572–573

Neset, Svanaug Olsdatter, II:204, 523, 539, 540; III:395, 397, 483, 523, 543, 565, 572–573, 579

Nesheim/Næsheim, Johannes Olson, I:174, 175, 176, 219, 390; II:108

Nesheim/Næsheim, John, II:108

Nesheim/Næsheim, Lars Nilsen/ Nielsen, I:174–175, 176, 219–220

Nesheim/Næsheim, Magrete Nilsdatter. *See* Heve/Hove, Magrete Nilsdatter

Nesheim/Næsheim, Martha Haldorsdatter, I:172, 174, 219–220, 240–241, 390, 392

Nesheim/Næsheim, Ole Johannesen, I:390

Nesheim/Næsheim, Synneve. *See* Folkedal, Synneve

Næsheim. *See* Nesheim/Næsheim

Nestegaard, Ole, III:129

Nesterud, Gunder Larsen, I:382

Netland, Ole Olsen, III:563–564

Neumann, Jacob, Bishop, I:48–49, 52–53, 55

Nevje, Professor, III:557, 558

Nielsen, Anders, I:145–146

Nielsen, Aslak, I:145–146

Nielsen, Daniel, I:352

Nielsen, Hans. *See* Gamkinn, Hans Nielsen

Nielsen, Margrith, I:149, 150

Nielsen, Mr., I:93

Nielsen, Theresia, III:94

Nieshiem, Mareta/Magrete Haldors Dater. *See* Nesheim/Næsheim, Martha Haldorsdatter

Nilsdatter, Gunhild Johanne (Nillie), II:378

Nilsdatter, Mari, I:359, 394

Nilsdatter, Sigrid, I:218, 245, 265, 337

Nilsen. *See also* Nelson

Nilsen, Amalie Pedersdatter, II:356

Nilsen, Anders, I:296; II:287

Nilsen, Astri, III:206

Nilsen, Erik, I:171

Nilsen, Evelyn Bergitte, III:138, 203

Nilsen, Even, II:531, 532; III:59, 60, 68

Nilsen, Gunhild Embriksdatter, I:171

Nilsen, Hans. *See* Fjære, Hans Nilsen; Lind, Hans Nilsen

Nilsen, Jens Antonius, II:456–457

Nilsen, Jokum, I:237

Nilsen, Kasper. *See* Fjære, Kasper Nilsen

Nilsen, Lars, III:179

Nilsen, Martha, III:260, 344

Nilsen, Mathea Kristoffersdatter, II:536, 537

Nilsen, Nils. *See* Gudmundsrud, Nils Nilsen

Nilsen, Olaf. *See* Nelson, Olaf

Nilsen, Ole, I:337; II:530, 531; III:145–146, 176, 179, 183, 202–203, 205, 218

Nilsen, Ole/Ola (Big), III:59, 60, 84, 97, 146, 205, 206, 215, 216

Nilsen, Ole/Ola (Little), III:60, 107, 109, 132, 146, 200

Nilsen, Peder, III:307

Nilsen, Sigrid O., III:59

Nilsen, Sigri N., II:532; III:59–60, 67–68, 83, 84, 144, 146, 178, 201, 531–532

Nilsen, Torjus, III:97

Noaas, Thosten Larsen, II:137

Nohr, Karl, III:591–592

Nomeland, Gunder, III:125, 126

Nomeland, Knut Jørgensen, III:125, 126

Nomeland, Olav, III:126

Nomeland, Ole Jørgensen, III:125, 126

Norby, Gulbrand, II:514

Norby, Halsten, I:228

Nordboe/Nordbø, Halvor, II:378, 439, 511

Nordboe/Nordbø, Johannes, I:88, 117, 118, 146
Nordboe/Nordbø, Nils, II:547
Nordbø. *See* Nordboe/Nordbø
Nordby, Inger, III:362, 455
Nordby, Jens S., III:361–362, 405–406, 454–455
Nordby, Syver, III:362, 455
Norderhus, Ole, II:219
Nordhagen, Torkel, II:544
Nordhus, Anne Andresen, II:126–127
Nordhus, Peder Mortensen, II:126–127
Nordmannsplassen/ Normandsplassen, Guri Helgesdatter, I:431; II:215
Nordmannsplassen/ Normandsplassen, Lars, II:215
Nordrum, Gunder Hansen, II:171, 350, 351–352, 434–435
Nordrum, Kari Mikkelsdatter, II:171, 351–352, 434–435
Nordt, Olaf, II:467, 468
Nordvik, Randi, II:309
Nordvolden, Helene, I:302
Nordvolden, Jacob, I:302
Norlie, O. M., II:86
Normandsplassen. *See* Nordmannsplassen/ Normandsplassen
Normann, Bjarne, III:377
Normann, Christine/Christina, II:295, 308, 309, 339
Normann, Henrik, II:88
Normann, Henry, II:309
Normann, Max, II:309
Normann, Stina, II:216, 425, 552; III:94

Norsby/Nørsteby/Nørstebø, Anne, II:324–325, 344–345, 431, 455–456, 479, 528, 538, 544; III:188–189
Norsby/Nørsteby/Nørstebø, Bjørner/Barney, II:429, 430, 477, 479, 548, 549; III:65, 151, 189, 190
Norsby/Nørsteby/Nørstebø, Jacob/ Jakob, II:324, 325, 431, 456, 479; III:65, 151, 188, 190, 229, 252
Norsby/Nørsteby/Nørstebø, Johannes, II:324, 325; II:478–479
Norsby/Nørsteby/Nørstebø, Marit, II:324, 431, 479; III:188, 251, 252
Norsby/Nørsteby/Nørstebø, Nelly, III:65
Norsby/Nørsteby/Nørstebø, Ole, III:65
Norsby/Nørsteby/Nørstebø, Rønnaug/Rine, II:325, 344, 429, 430, 431, 455, 456, 477, 479, 543. *See also* Huslegard/ Huslegarden, Rønnaug/Rine
Norsby/Nørsteby/Nørstebø, Sivert, II:324, 325, 344, 429, 431, 455, 456, 477, 479; III:65
Noss, Guri, II:531
Noss, Ingebjør/Ingeborg, III:83, 84, 97, 98
Noss, Lars Larsen, III:84, 98
Nygaard, Kristi, III:360
Nygaard, Ole, II:253
Nygaardslien, Gudmund, I:105
Nystul, Ole, I:100–101
Nystøl, Mikal Hendrik, I:393
Nysæter, Gullik Olson, III:85
Næs, Ole H., I:187

Næss. *See* Naess/Næss

Nørsteby/Nørstebø. *See* Norsby/
  Nørsteby/Nørstebø

Nøttestadvangen, Edvard Evensen,
  III:373–374, 431, 456, 466–
  467, 486, 523, 532–533, 553–
  554, 587, 589–590, 599–600,
  623

Nøttestadvangen, Even Eriksen,
  III:422

Nøttestadvangen, Marte
  Rasmusdatter, III:373–374,
  431, 456, 466–467, 486,
  523, 532–533, 553–554, 587,
  589–590, 599–600, 623

Oftedal, Fredrik, I:55; II:132

Oftedal, Henrik Hanson, II:402

Oftedal, Sven, III:97

Ohnstad/Onstad, Regine, III:427–
  428

Ohnstad/Onstad, Roggine,
  III:430–431

Ohnstad/Onstad family, III:427

Olausen, Hans, II:562

Oline, Anna/Annie, II:130, 359,
  497

Olsdatter, Anne, III:81. *See also*
  Opsata, Anne Olsdatter

Olsdatter, Birgit, II:532

Olsdatter, Inger, I:260

Olsdatter, Ingrid, I:448

Olsdatter, Karoline, III:535

Olsdatter, Kirsti, I:238, 239

Olsdatter, Margit, III:238–239

Olsdatter, Synneva, I:185

Olsdatter, Tone, I:356, 358;
  II:307–308, 309

Olsdatter, Torand, I:286–287

Olsen. *See also* Olson

Olsen, Anders, II:359

Olsen, Andreas, II:206

Olsen, Anna Kristine, III:167–168

Olsen, Bør, I:237, 239

Olsen, C., II:467

Olsen, Carl, III:621

Olsen, Carl E., III:493

Olsen, Elling, I:285, 286. *See also*
  Elsrud, Elling Olsen

Olsen, Gullik. *See* Østern, Gullik
  Olsen

Olsen, Halvor, I:97

Olsen, Hans, I:81. *See also*
  Thomter, Hans Olsen

Olsen, Helleik. *See* Lehovd,
  Hellik/Helleik Olson/Olsen

Olsen, Ingebret, III:167–168

Olsen, Jacob. *See* Østern, Jacob/
  Jakob Olsen

Olsen, Jakob, III:128

Olsen, Josefine, II:491, 542, 562

Olsen, Karen/Carrie/Kay/Kai/Kye
  Olsdatter, II:412, 413, 443

Olsen, Katie/Kristine, III:157–158

Olsen, Knud. *See* Ringnes, Knud
  Olsen

Olsen, Kristine. *See* Nelp, Kristine
  Olsdatter

Olsen, Lars. *See* Huset, Lars Olsen

Olsen, Marie, III:167–168

Olsen, Martin, III:302

Olsen, Michael, I:147

Olsen, Mina Gropa, III:114, 115

Olsen, Mons, I:260

Olsen, Mr., III:497–498

Olsen, Mr., II:29

Olsen, Olaus, II:380, 444, 562

Olsen, Ole, III:238–239

Olsen, Svend, I:336, 337

Olsen, Torgrim. *See* Haugerud,
  Torgrim Olsen

Olsen, Torje. *See* Solberg, Torje Olsen

Olsen, Viking, I:177

Olsen/Olson, K, I:88, 89, 93

Olsen/Olson, Nels/Nils Torvetjønn, II:204–205, 217–218, 304, 522–523, 539–540; III:238–239, 255–256, 397, 494–495, 522–523, 542–543, 564–565, 572–573, 578–579

Olsen/Olson, Ole, I:105, 297, 322–323; II:537. *See also* Haugerud, Ole Olsen; Heve/Hove, Ole Olsen/Olson; Lehovd, Ole Olsen/Olson

Olshullet, Beret Olsdatter, I:233

Olson. *See also* Olsen

Olson, Anne Vetlesdatter, II:523

Olson, Erick G., III:356, 367–368, 516–517, 520–521, 574–575. *See also* Goderstad, Erik Olsen

Olson, Gisle, III:396, 397

Olson, Hellik. *See* Lehovd, Hellik/Helleik Olson/Olsen

Olson, Ingebrigt H., II:375, 384–385

Olson, Jakob/Jacob, II:103–104, 345, 367–368, 456, 458–459, 479, 538, 549; III:140, 151–152, 188, 229

Olson, Karen, II:375–376, 384–385, 455, 456, 458, 491–492; III:110, 140

Olson, Nels/Nils T. *See* Olsen/Olson, Nels/Nils Torvetjønn

Olson, Ole, II:538; III:188, 229

Olson, Ole G., III:516, 575

Olson, Ole T., III:483

Olson, Olianna, II:103–104, 458. *See also* Hanson, Olianna

Olson, Ragnhild/Rena/Ragnhilld, II:543–544, 548, 549, 553, 554; III:65, 139, 140, 189, 191, 229. *See also* Vigerust, Ragnhild Olsdatter

Olson, T. *See* Ødegaard, Ole Tobias Olsen

Olson, Tor, II:523

Olstad, Ole, I:189; II:270, 363

Omodt, Mr., III:184

Omodt, Mrs., III:184

Omsrud, Anne, II:483

Omsrud, Oline, II:483

Onsager, Andrew, III:98, 179

Onsager, Guri, III:97, 98, 179

Onstad, Regina, II:362

Opedal, Svend Iverson, II:156

Opheim, Halvor Knutsen, I:453

Opheim, Randi Tollefsdatter, I:317, 349–350; II:50–51, 135, 175

Opheim, Sevat Bøjrnsen, II:51

Opheimsjordet, Arne Olson, I:154

Oppedal, Iver, II:145

Opper, Fredrick Burr, III:306

Oprud, Christian, II:253

Opsata, Aagot, I:361, 452; II:137

Opsata, Anne Olsdatter, I:263, 362, 453; II:391

Opsata, Haagen/Haakon Tollefsen, I:317, 360, 362, 451; II:51, 134, 135, 175

Opsata, Kari Tollefsdatter, I:317

Opsata, Margit Olsdatter, I:317, 361; II:51, 137, 138; III:130, 177, 179, 234

Opsata, Niels, I:362; II:137

Opsata, Nils Tollefsen, I:316, 317

Opsata, Ole Tollefsen/Tellefsen, I:317, 349, 350, 360, 362, 453; II:51, 135, 136, 137–138

Opsata, Sigri, I:361
Opsata, Thorsten, II:137
Opsata, Tollef, I:362, 452; II:137
Opsata, Tosten, I:361, 452
Orwoll, Sylvester Martinus, III:526, 527
Os, Karl Isaksen, III:74
Oscar II, King, III:407–408
Osland, Andreas, I:321
Osland, Anne, I:66–67
Osland, Halsten, I:67
Osland, Hellik, I:67
Osland, Herbrand Paulsen, I:107, 108, 179, 182–183, 194, 208
Osland, Knut, I:67
Osland, Ole Herbrandsen, I:66–67, 106–107, 108, 182
Osland, Ole Olsen, I:396
Osnes, Martin, II:123
Osterhaus, Lina, II:278
Osterhaus, Ludvig, II:277, 278
Osuldsen, Peder, III:156–157
Otilie, Maren, I:197
Ottesen, Jacob Aal, I:320–321, 323
Ovedahl/Ovedal. *See also* Allikson; Aslakson
Ovedal, Barbro Sigbjørnsdatter, II:182
Ovedal, Beren/Berent/Bernt Andreas Atlaksen, I:346, 392, 393, 394, 405, 406, 414–415; II:56; III:81
Ovedal, Berte/Berthe Tonette/Tonnette Larsdatter, II:56, 298, 299, 403; III:82, 193, 235, 244–245, 252–253, 253–254
Ovedal, Bolette, II:403, 482, 555, 556; III:82

Ovedal, Haavard/Haavar/Haaver/Hover Sigbjørnsen, I:342; II:182, 281, 556
Ovedal, Henrik, II:195
Ovedal, Ingeborg, II:403, 482, 555, 556; III:82
Ovedal, Karen Tonette, I:347; II:182, 195, 556
Ovedal, Osmund Atlaksen/Atlakson, I:165–166, 210, 324–325, 341–342, 346, 392, 393, 394, 405, 407, 414–415; II:55–56, 68–69, 74–75, 91–92, 94–95, 100–101, 113–114, 131–132, 181–182, 194–195, 280–281, 298, 299, 402–403, 481–482, 555–556; III:81–82, 193, 209–210, 213–214, 217, 235
Ovedal, Osmund Gabrielsen, I:342, 393
Ovedal, Sara Atlaksdatter, I:346, 347, 392, 393, 394
Ovedal, Sigbjørn Haaverson, II:195
Ovedal, Siri Gabrielsdatter, I:342, 347, 393, 394
Ovedal, Trond/Tron Haaversen, I:414, 415
Overland, Tarjulv, III:364
Ovstanes/Ystanes, Jacob Mikkelsen, III:448, 449

Paalsen. *See also* Paulsen
Paalsen, Hellik. *See* Aasland, Hellik Paalsen
Paalsen, Herbran/Herbrand. *See* Osland, Herbrand Paulsen
Paaske, Frithjof, III:485

Pabst, Ingeborg, II:37, 38, 88, 308, 309, 339, 346, 347, 398, 426, 453, 454, 504; III:92–93, 95, 96, 99, 100. *See also* Bache, Mrs.

Pabst, Oscar, II:37, 38

Palmesen, Fingal, II:514

Parnell, Charles Stuart, II:293, 294

Paulsen. *See also* Paalsen

Paulsen, Agnete, II:277

Paulsen, Halvor, I:398

Paulsen, Herbran/Herbrand. *See* Osland, Herbrand Paulsen

Paulsen, John, I:146, 148

Paulsen, Marit Helgesdatter, I:398

Paulsen, Ole, I:229

Pedersen. *See also* Pederson

Pedersen, Albrekt, III:283

Pedersen, Alette, III:473, 480

Pedersen, Anders, I:287, 288; II:127; III:473–474, 480, 529, 550, 581–582

Pedersen, Emil Johan, III:474

Pedersen, Hans, I:384; III:473. *See also* Kulpen, Hans Pedersen

Pedersen, Johan, I:287, 288; III:283

Pedersen, Johannes, III:474

Pedersen, Karen, III:473, 479, 480

Pedersen, Karoline/Kalla, III:479, 480, 529

Pedersen, Kristian/Christian, III:472, 473, 474, 479–480, 528, 529, 549–550, 581–582

Pedersen, Morten, II:127

Pedersen, Ole, II:359

Pedersen, Severin, III:480

Pederson. *See also* Pedersen

Pederson, Martin A., III:433–434, 469, 488–489

Peerson, Cleng, I:146, 340

Petersen, Edvard, III:537

Peterson, Aase Elene, III:575

Peterson, Anna, III:574, 575

Peterson, Karl, III:340, 341. *See also* Falla/Fella, Karl

Peterson, Torje, III:575

Pettersen, Lorenz, III:468

Pettersen, Martin. *See* Pederson, Martin A.

Pettersen, Masine, III:468

Pettersen, Peter, I:185

Petterson, Holger. *See* Helle, Holger Petterson

Pilrud, Ketil, II:423

Plassen, Anne, II:530; III:77, 108, 177, 180, 199

Plassen, Tore, II:530

Plath, Margaret, III:535

Plath, Sofie, III:535

Ploien, Mrs., III:479

Poppe, Karen/Kaja, I:352, 358, 375, 409, 411, 412, 449; II:87–88, 89, 90, 216, 297, 339, 340, 452, 454

Porsmyr, Andreas O., II:511

Post, C. W., III:489

Poulson, Poul, I:427, 428

Powers, John O'Connor, II:293, 294

Preus, Adolph Carl, I:176, 177

Preus, Christian Keyser, III:613, 615

Preus, Herman, A., I:211, 464, 466; II:28, 29, 132

Qvestad, Anne, I:145, 148, 149

Qvileqval, John Haldorsen, I:177

Raa, Jan, II:432

Raaen, Lars, I:191

Raaom, Helena Olsdatter, I:234
Rail, Maggie, II:123
Ramberg, Siri, I:107, 108
Ramstad, Anne, III:195
Ramstad, Ole, II:423, 475
Rannestad, Albert, II:195, 281,
    555; III:193
Rannestad, Alexander, II:181, 182
Rannestad, Asbjørn, II:113
Rannestad, John/Jon Torkelsen/
    Thorkelson, II:113, 114,
    131–132, 181, 182, 280–281,
    299, 481, 482; III:82, 193
Rannestad, Kolbjørn Pedersen,
    II:555
Rannestad, Ole Torkelsen/
    Thorkelson, II:113, 131, 132,
    481, 482
Rannestad, Osmund, III:253
Rannestad, Rakel/Rachel Tonette/
    Tonnette Thorkelson, II:113–
    114, 131, 132, 181–182, 194,
    195, 281, 298, 299, 481, 482,
    555–556; III:81, 82, 193,
    252–253, 254
Rannestad, Steffen Gabriel, II:281
Rannestad, Theodore/Theodor
    Christian, II:131, 132, 181, 195,
    481, 555; III:193
Rannestad, Tore, II:131
Rasmussen, Christian, II:425, 426;
    III:349, 554
Rasmussen, Johan. See Bjørgum,
    Johan Rasmusen/Rasmussen
Rasmussen, John, II:376
Rasmussen, Ludvig, III:240, 338,
    339, 348, 349, 374, 458, 467,
    525, 554, 589, 590, 625
Rasmussen, Ole, II:385; III:240,
    339, 374, 422, 487, 488, 525,
    533, 554, 589, 590, 625

Rasmussen, Peter Andreas, I:252,
    254, 255, 284, 356, 358
Rasmussen, Ramus, III:422
Rasmussen, Randi/Rangdi,
    III:338, 399, 457, 458, 466,
    487, 488, 525, 533, 554, 590,
    625
Rasmussen, Svein, II:436
Rasmussen, Svend, III:352
Ravn, Dr., III:182
Rebrud, Ingebor Olsdatter, I:277
Refshol, Edvard, III:498
Refshus, Even, III:281
Reiersdatter, Sigri/Sigrid, I:389;
    II:42, 58, 87
Reiersen, Alice, II:340
Reiersen, Andrew, I:94
Reiersen, C., I:450
Reiersen, Carl, I:94; II:37
Reiersen, Caroline Amalie (Lina).
    See Vinzent, Lina (Caroline
    Amalie)
Reiersen, Christian, I:89, 94, 112,
    358
Reiersen, G., I:89
Reiersen, Georg, I:94, 354, 355,
    376
Reiersen, Georgine, I:94
Reiersen, Gerhard, I:94
Reiersen, Gina, I:94
Reiersen, Helene, I:247, 248, 273,
    354, 376; II:38, 39, 398
Reiersen, Jens, I:94
Reiersen, Johan Heinrich (step-
    son), I:449; II:39, 340, 504
Reiersen, Johan Reinhert (J. R.),
    I:64, 86–87, 88, 90, 91–92, 93,
    94, 109, 112, 117, 145, 146,
    147, 149, 247, 248, 352–353,
    358, 375, 403; II:39, 339, 340;
    III:70, 96

Reiersen, Kristian Severin, II:340

Reiersen, Lassen, I:87, 94, 354;
II:38

Reiersen, Lina. *See* Vinzent, Lina
(Caroline Amalie)

Reiersen, Mathilde, I:354

Reiersen, Ole Johan, I:94, 354,
376, 449; II:88, 89

Reiersen, Oscar, I:353, 358, 376;
II:425, 498

Reiersen, Ouline, I:247, 248, 353,
354, 358, 376, 410, 449, 450;
II:37, 38, 39, 88, 297, 339, 340,
346–347, 396, 397, 426, 452,
453, 454, 498, 504, 533, 552;
III:70, 71, 93, 94, 96, 100,
111–112, 113

Reiersen, Peder/Peter Georg, I:248,
273; II:38, 39

Reiersen, Sigurd, I:376; II:37–38

Reiersen, Thomas, I:354–355

Reinton, Ole Syverson, I:199

Reinton, S., III:104

Reinton, Sigurd Olsen, III:103,
104, 105

Reisland, Elling Helgesen, I:431;
II:215

Relling, I. T., II:307, 309

Rene, Knut A., II:121

Ribe, Eliot, III:309, 310, 312

Ribrud, John, I:214

Riddervold, Hans, I:146

Rigstad, Marit, III:272, 437

Ringen, Hans, III:108

Ringen, Randi, III:266, 281

Ringnes, Johan, II:70

Ringnes, Knud Olsen, I:112, 118,
144, 145, 146, 149, 259

Ringnes, Mrs., II:70

Ringstad, Pastor, III:129

Rise, Anne, II:345

Rise, Ole, II:506

Rise, Tore, II:355

Ro, Ole, I:362

Roa, Reier Olsen, I:112

Roberts, Oran M., Governor,
III:99, 101

Rodney. *See* Rødne/Rodney

Rodningsand, Ole H., II:25, 80,
81

Roe, Kari Tollefsdatter, I:63, 65

Roe, Nils Tollefsen, I:65

Roe, Ole, II:174

Rogne, Ole Larson, I:215–216,
217

Rogstad, Anna Marthea, I:380;
II:183

Rogstad, Anne Eriksdatter, I:150,
380, 403, 427, 455; II:111, 116,
227, 259, 348, 377, 465

Rogstad, Berger Tollevsen, I:150,
380–381, 455; II:111, 116, 227

Rogstad, Bernt/Berendt Adolf,
I:380; II:348

Rogstad, Johan, I:380; II:275–276

Rogstad, Perine Pouline, I:380

Rogstad, Thomas Renhart, I:380

Romestvedt, Ole, I:55

Romestvedt, Peder, I:55

Roosevelt, Theodore, President,
III:334, 337, 339, 349, 509, 557,
558

Rornes, Hans Christian, II:33

Rosenkilde, Bendix, II:454

Rosenkilde family, II:89, 426, 454

Rosenvold family, II:454

Rossing, Ole O., II:247, 248,
248–249, 276

Rossum, Brede, I:368

Rostad, O. H., II:467

Rothe/Røthe, Martha, III:584,
594

Rothe/Røthe, Peter/Per Svendsen, III:327, 328, 420–421, 449, 545–546, 583–584, 594
Rothe/Røthe, Svein, III:585
Roti, Lars Larsen, II:395
Rotnemsjeøn, Halgrim, I:155
Rovold, Kari, II:389
Rud, Kristofer, II:312
Rudi, Anna, II:430
Rudi, Johan, III:88
Rue, Halvor Syversen, I:448
Rue, Kitil Eriksen, I:155–156, 158
Rue, Maren Kathrine, I:448
Rue, Syver O., I:447, 448
Ruenæs, Pastor, II:488
Rundhaug, Gudbrand/Gulbrand, II:513–514; III:360, 361, 406, 454
Rundhaug, Torgrim Olsen, III:285
Runhaug, Fingal, II:362, 432
Runhaug, Guri, II:362
Runhaug, Thorvald, II:362
Russell, I:119
Russell, Nella, I:119
Russell, Peter, I:119
Rust, Hans O., I:361, 362
Rustad, Lars Olsen, II:180
Rustand, Beret Olsdatter, I:233
Rustand, Eric, I:231, 232
Rustand, Guri Torgrimsdatter, I:233, 265, 278, 280, 288, 290, 435, 441–442; II:25, 81, 140
Rustand, Hans Olsen, I:232, 233, 260
Rustand, Inger Olsdatter, I:260
Rustand, Ole (the elder). See Haugerud, Ole Olsen (the elder)
Rustand, Ole (the younger). See Haugerud, Ole Olsen (the younger)

Rustand, Ole Hansen, I:232–233, 259–260, 280, 435, 442
Rustand, Olia, I:233
Ruste, Kristofer, II:558; III:607
Ruste, Tidemann, II:558; III:607
Rustebakke, Amund, II:545
Rusten, Even, III:348
Ruud, Martin B., I:323
Ryan, S. O., III:227
Rykkhus, Ole Olsen, II:179, 180
Ryngom, E. A., III:543
Rynning, Ole, I:55, 59
Rysjubraaten, Anders, III:361
Rystad, Bergitte. See Knudsen, Bergitte
Rystad, John, II:358
Rystad, Jon/John Knutsen, II:309, 454
Rystad, Pastor, II:552
Rødde, Sivert, III:64
Rødne/Rodney, Haldor, III:620–621
Rødne/Rodney, Ole, III:350, 359
Rødne/Rodney, Severin, III:411
Rødningen, Erland Olsen, I:104, 105
Rødningen, Marthe Rasmusdatter, I:104, 105
Rødningen, Ole, I:104
Røgenes, Nikolay, III:621
Røiland, Tønnes, III:470
Rømcke, Dr., III:182
Rønningsand, Jon, I:425
Rønningsdalen, Ole Olsen/Olson, I:386, 437
Rønvik/Rønvig, Richard Pedersen, III:284, 299, 300, 315, 318, 319, 325, 356–357, 377, 389, 390, 394
Rørtvedt, Cornelius, III:206

Rørvig, Britha/Brita Olsdatter, I:326, 330
Rørvig, Ole, I:330
Røthe. *See* Rothe/Røthe
Røtterud, Ellen, III:259

Saga, Christine Carlsdatter, I:302
Saga, Lars Olsen, I:301, 302
Sagen, Knut, III:181
Sagvolden, Margit, II:174
Salvesen/Salveson, Ole, II:555–556
Salvesen/Salveson, Tønnes, II:39
Sand, Kari, I:232
Sand, Karoline, I:425
Sandbakken, Anne, II:287
Sandehuset, Margrete. *See* Kristiansen, Margrete
Sandell, Lina, II:429
Sandestølen, Ingeborg, III:77
Sandestølen, Margit, II:530; III:108, 177, 205
Sandhuset, Fredrik, III:84
Sando, Barbro Tollefsdatter/ Tolleivsdatter, I:63, 65, 316–317, 349–350, 362, 452, 453; II:50–51, 135–136, 173–174, 174–175
Sando, Berthe Maria, I:317; II:50, 135, 174–175
Sando, Erik O., I:65, 349, 362; II:50
Sando, Gjermund, I:349; II:50, 174
Sando, Gustav Adolph, II:134–135
Sando, Halvor Olsen, I:349; II:50, 51
Sando, Lars Eriksen, I:349; II:50, 51
Sando, Ole Eriksen, I:65, 317, 362; II:135, 175
Sando, Ole Olsen, I:452, 453; II:134, 135–136, 138

Sando, Tollef, I:349, 362; II:50
Sandsmark, Berte, I:414
Sandsmark, Tobias, I:414
Sandvig. *See also* Sandvik
Sandvig, Mrs., III:264, 282
Sandvig family, III:276–277
Sandvik. *See also* Sandvig
Sandvik, Gyrid Jakobsdatter, II:526
Sandvik, Jakob/Jacob Rasmussen, II:143, 146, 148–149, 155–156, 197–198, 251–252, 300–301, 321, 333, 360–361, 403, 405, 435, 437, 469–470, 473–474, 524, 526; III:72, 295, 351–352, 540–541, 585
Sandvik, Kari Aamundsdatter, II:264–265
Sandvik, Nils, II:547
Sandvik, Rasmus Svendsen, II:470, 474, 526
Sandvik, Svend Rasmusen, II:149, 252, 264–265, 301, 333
Sandvik, Torbjørg, I:156; II:470
Sandvik, Torine, II:225
Sanvig. *See* Sandvik
Sartz, Richard Sophus Nilsen, III:613, 615
Satalien, Guri, III:130
Sataslaatta, Guri Olsdatter, I:65
Schare. *See* Skare
Schimling/Skimling, Kristian Larsen, III:350
Schjølberg, R. M. B., III:306, 307, 401
Schjøth, Alvilde/Alvhilde, I:271, 272, 371
Schjøth, Anton, I:246, 248, 273, 355, 371
Schjøth, Anton Christian Rudolf, I:371

Skadeland, Halvor Gundersen, I:203, 419, 443; II:49, 141

Skalshaug, Ole, I:229

Skamfer, Marit, III:276

Skardet, Thore, II:312

Skare, Anders Helgesen, I:203–204, 225–226, 305–306, 315, 318–319, 408, 445; II:90–91, 140–141, 194, 220, 221–222

Skare, Eli Andersdatter, I:151, 203–204

Skare, Eli Helgesdatter, I:310–311, 418–419, 445

Skare, Elly, II:144

Skare, Gunder Helgesen, I:153, 291, 292, 310, 311, 314, 315–316, 318–319, 407–408, 419; II:49–50, 82, 194, 306

Skare, Halvor Helgesen, I:292, 305, 316, 318–319, 408, 419, 431, 443; II:82, 90–91, 140–141, 215, 307

Skare, Helge Gundersen, I:151, 203–204, 225–226, 290, 292, 303, 310–311, 314, 315–316, 318–319, 407–408, 418–419, 429, 431, 443, 444–445; II:48, 50, 81–82, 90–91, 140–141, 193–194, 214–215, 220–221, 221–222, 306–307. *See also* Gundersen, Helge

Skare, Ingeborg Helgesdatter, I:203, 204, 225–226, 292, 311, 314–315, 319. *See also* Evensen, Ingeborg Helgesdatter

Skare, Ingrid Helgesdatter, I:152–53, 203, 204, 419

Skare, Jakob Gulbrandsen, I:305

Skare, Mari/Marit/Margit Helgesdatter, I:151–152, 152–153, 203, 204, 292, 311, 398, 443; II:307

Skareeie, Lars Olsen, I:204

Skareeie, Ole Eriksen, I:204

Skari, Lise, I:369, 370

Skarsbø, Karen, III:568

Skeie, Neri, III:237

Skeie, Thor. *See* Vigenstad, Tor/Thor Torstensen

Skibeli, Hendrik/Henrik, I:393; II:403

Skibeli, Olene, I:341–342

Skibeli, Siri, I:341–342

Skillebekk, Anton Larsen, I:257, 301

Skillebekk, Maren Larsen, I:257, 258, 302

Skimling/Schimling, T., III:359

Skindingsrud boys, I:228

Skinningsrud, Anders, II:382–383, 441

Skinningsrud, Ingeborg, II:312

Skinningsrud, Østen, II:284, 312

Skjeldal, Klaus Knutsen, I:219, 220

Skjerpe, Hans, I:393; II:482

Skjerpe, Jendal, I:393

Skjerpe, Marte, II:482

Skjerven/Skjervheim, Lars, III:129, 130, 131, 180

Skjerven/Skjervheim, Sissel, III:129, 130, 131

Skjolden, John/Johan, II:499, 503

Skjong, Christian, III:234

Skjulstad, Martha, III:167, 168

Skjæveland, Ole Olsen, I:296, 297

Skogehagen, Knut, III:126

Skogehagen, Ole, III:126

Skogehagen, Tor, III:126

Skottebøl, Aagot Tollefsdatter,
    I:317

Skottebøl family, I:316

Skrattegard, Lars Larsen, I:337,
    423

Skrattegard, Ole L., III:68

Skrattegard, Ole Svendsen, III:177

Skrattegard, Sigri, III:83, 84, 98

Skrattegard, Svend Olsen, I:336,
    337

Skrefsrud, Lars, III:93, 96

Skria/Skrien, Anne T., III:177,
    181, 223

Skria/Skrien, Guri T., III:97, 98,
    107, 181

Skrinde, Ole Olsen, I:63

Skrovik, Ole, II:470

Skrovik, Torbjørg, II:470

Slagsvold, Ottine, II:105, 106

Slette, Johannes, II:368

Slette, Mari, II:345

Slette, Mattias, III:190

Slette, Ole, II:368

Slettebratten, Knud, I:378

Slimsen, Eric, I:232

Smedal, Aslak, III:453

Smedal, Gunleik, III:453

Smidt, Johan Gustaf/Gustav, I:53,
    55

Smith, Eli, III:614–615

Smith, Emilie Josefine, III:614

Smith, Ernst Hadeler, III:614

Smith, Magna, III:612

Smith, Major, I:54

Smith, Mr., I:87

Smith, Mr., III:184, 197

Snausen, Karen Karlsdatter, II:391

Snekkerlia/Snekkerlien. *See also*
    Lee/Lie

Snekkerlia/Snekkerlien, Andreas
    Olsen, II:548–549. *See also* Lee/
    Lie, Anders Olsen

Snekkerlia/Snekkerlien, Anne/Ane,
    II:458–459, 538, 544, 549, 543,
    544, 554; III:150–151, 187, 188

Snekkerlia/Snekkerlien, Hans,
    III:65; III:190

Snekkerlia/Snekkerlien, Ole Olsen,
    II:324, 325, 368, 458–459;
    III:151

Snidkerlien, Andrias. *See* Lee/
    Lie, Anders/Andrew/Andreas/
    Andrias

Sogn, Torsten, I:369, 370

Solberg, Carl Edward, III:422

Solberg, Christian/Kristian
    Edvardsen, III:374, 404–405,
    421–422, 432–433, 487–488,
    525, 532–533, 589–590, 625

Solberg, Even Edvardsen, III:239–
    240, 339–340, 348–349,
    373–374, 404–405, 421–422,
    524–525, 553–554, 588–589,
    599–600, 625

Solberg, Karen Torjesdatter,
    III:516–517, 520–521, 574–575

Solberg, Laura, III:374, 405, 486,
    488

Solberg, Ole Edvardsen, III:457–
    458, 466–467, 525, 625

Solberg, Pastor, II:169, 172

Solberg, Torje Olsen, III:289–290,
    355–356, 367–368, 521, 575

Solem. *See also* Ødegaard

Solem, Alma, III:526–527

Solem, Arne, I:155

Solem, Carl, II:320, 413, 443, 462,
    541, 560, 562

Solem, Christian, II:320, 413,
428–429, 443, 462, 560, 562;
III:196, 198
Solem, Clara, III:61
Solem, Johan, II:413, 462, 512,
540, 560, 562; III:196
Solem, Karen, II:320, 355–356,
389–390, 412–413, 427–428,
429, 443–444, 461–462,
466, 467–468, 490–491, 509,
512–513, 536–537, 541–542,
562; III:62–63, 116, 133,
135, 185–186, 198, 220–221,
248–249, 260, 340–341, 344
Solem, Karl, II:428–429; III:186,
196, 198
Solem, Louis/Lauris/Laurits
Nilsen, II:320–321, 355–356,
390, 428–429, 443, 461, 462,
509, 512, 513, 534, 535, 536,
540, 561; III:62, 114, 134, 135,
184, 196, 219, 249, 342–343
Solem, Marie, II:412, 413, 443,
461, 466, 467, 509, 541, 542;
III:62, 115, 116, 197, 198, 342,
343, 344, 475–476
Solem, Mina, II:490, 508, 509,
512, 536, 540; III:116. *See also*
Kjønstad, Mina
Solem, Nicolai/Nikolai, II:320,
390, 428–429, 442, 443, 461,
462, 490, 508, 512, 536, 540,
561, 562; III:61, 62, 114, 116
Solem, Nils Christophersen,
II:320, 321, 428–429, 462
Solem, Nordt, III:527
Solem, Olaus, II:428–429, 442,
443, 461, 462; III:114, 116
Solem, Olga, III:61, 134, 197, 478,
527
Solem family, II:321

Solheim, Syvert, III:364
Solvi, Tomas, I:184
Song, Anders A., II:351
Song, Mari, II:351
Songe, Gjeruld, I:187
Songe, Johanne Svenningsdatter/
Sveningsdatter, I:186–187,
209–210, 211–212
Songe, Thor, I:187
Sorensen/Sørensen, Andreas,
I:265; II:139
Sorensen/Sørensen, Marie, III:493,
557
Sorensen/Sørensen, Mathilde J.,
I:356
Sorensen/Sørensen, Mrs., II:397,
398; III:94
Sorensen/Sørensen, Terje, I:186
Sortbekken, Hendrik, I:191
Sorteberg. *See also* Hjallo
Sorteberg, E., III:180
Sortebraaten, Gulbrand, II:253
Spangen, Jørgen Christophersen,
I:450
Speilberg, Christian G., II:398;
III:94, 96
Speilberg, Lotte, II:89
Sperati, Carlo Alberto, III:613,
615
Spikes, Ophelia Florence, II:37,
347
Spikes, Ovie, II:347
Spilde, Johannes Iversen, II:479,
480–481
Staack, James Hendrik, I:93, 145,
150
Stabekk, Clement, I:201
Stabo, Trond, III:613, 615
Stafnehaug, Arnt, III:281
Stampen, Jacob, II:29
Stampen, Johannes, II:29

Strømstad, Gitle Torgersen, II:403, 482

Stub, Hans Andreas, I:98, 104, 105, 210

Stub, Hans Gerhard (and Mrs.), III:613, 615

Stuga, Sofie, III:581

Stugaarden/Stugarden, Harald, I:229, 439–440, 441

Stugaarden/Stugarden, Jakob Olsen, I:379

Stykop, Niri Sjulsen, I:234

Støa, Anton, III:454

Støa, T., III:360

Suby, Stenner, III:76

Sumbren, Birgit, III:181

Sumbren, Ole E., II:531

Sund, Engebret, II:407

Sund, Ole, II:475; III:195

Sund, Peder, III:284

Sundre, Guri, II:530

Sundre, Johan, III:180

Sundre, Kari, II:531; III:59, 60, 84

Sundre, Lars, II:530

Sundre, Margit, II:530

Sundt, John, III:305

Sunne, Ole Pedersen, II:542, 562

Sutter, Mr., I:126

Svadde, Engebret/Ingebrigt Østensen, I:97, 98

Svartekjær, Lars, III:290

Svedjan, Hans, III:174

Svee, Marit Jonsdatter, II:460

Sveen, Anders, II:434

Sveen, Christian, I:105

Sveen, Johan, II:460; III:243

Sveen, Jørgen, II:460

Sveinson, John, II:437

Svenagsen, Ole, I:78

Svenagsen, Thor, I:78

Svendsdatter, Gunhild, I:158

Svendsdatter, Sigrid, II:470

Svendsen, Albert, III:68, 76

Svendsen, Andreas, I:377

Svendsen, Aslak Johan, II:361–362

Svendsen, Aslaug Andersdatter, II:168

Svendsen, Birgit, II:530, 532; III:59, 60, 77, 83, 108, 179, 216

Svendsen, Faste, III:519, 520

Svendsen, Gro, I:200, 337, 532; III:60, 84, 98, 146, 179

Svendsen, Ingeborg, III:98

Svendsen, Jacob/Jakob, II:252, 362

Svendsen, Mrs., III:259

Svendsen, Niels, II:531

Svendsen, Nils O., III:60, 68, 77, 83, 84, 97, 98, 107, 108, 131, 146, 181, 198, 199, 206, 215, 216, 218, 223, 224, 233–234

Svendsen, Ole O., I:337; II:532; III:59, 60, 68, 77, 83, 84, 130, 179, 180, 224

Svendsen, Paul, II:168

Svendsen, Sevat, III:98, 130

Svendsen, Sigri, III:76–77, 83–84, 97–98, 109, 129, 131–132, 146, 176, 178–179, 181, 183, 200, 201, 205–206, 215–216, 218, 223–224, 234

Svendsen, Svend. See Erfjord, Svend Svendsen

Svendsen, Tragethon, III:205

Svendson/Svensen, John. See Svenson/Svensen/Swenson, John

Sveningsen, Mogens/Mons, I:208, 209–210

Svennungsen, Stener, III:221

Svensen, O., I:403, 405

Svenson/Svensen/Swenson, John, II:361–362, 405, 436–437, 473–474; III:260

Svensrud, Anne Hansdatter, I:290

Sverdrup, Edvard, III:519, 520

Swanson, Jacob, II:362

Swenson. *See* Svendsen

Swenson, John. *See* Svenson/
Svensen/Swenson, John

Syftestad, Olaus Paulsen, II:441,
442

Syl, Ingebor-Anna, I:236

Syl, Nils Mikkelsen, I:205, 236

Syl, Simen, I:236

Syversdatter, Kari, I:124

Syversen, Karen, II:517

Syversen, S., II:329

Syversen, Sofie, III:260

Syversen, Syver, III:258

Sæther, Mr. and Mrs., III:258

Sætra/Sætre, Gulbrand, I:214

Sætra/Sætre, Hans, I:393

Sætra/Sætre, Ole Gulbrandsen,
I:328

Sætra/Sætre, Ole Sjurson, I:172,
177

Sævig, Torbjørn, I:209

Søberg, Fredrik, III:423

Søggar, Einar, III:281

Søggar, Lars, III:281

Søggard, Johanne, III:386

Søland, Ole Embrektson, II:82

Søli, Allethe, I:401

Søli, Allette Olsdatter, II:129, 232,
234, 319

Sølibakken, Rønnaug, I:229

Sørensen. *See* Sorensen/Sørensen

Sørflaaten/Sørflaten, Harald,
III:375, 531

Sørli/Sørlie, Harald, II:483;
III:232

Sørli/Sørlie, Kari, II:172; III:562,
563

Sørli/Sørlie, Mikkel Mikkelsen,
II:171, 172, 274, 312, 314, 351,
435, 558; III:230, 232, 246,
562, 563, 607, 611

Sørli/Sørlie, Oline, II:351, 483;
III:461

Sørli/Sørlie, Ragnhild Olsdatter,
II:312, 351, 435

Sørli/Sørlie, Tidemand, III:461

Sørum, Anne, III:416

Sørum, Simon Hansen, I:232, 233

Søstuen, Ole, III:338, 348

Taarudmoen, Jesper, III:190

Taarvig, Christopher, I:356

Tackle, Johannes, II:145

Taft, William Howard, President,
III:450, 557, 558, 596

Taksdal, Ole Jesperson, I:297

Takserud, Hellik, I:396, 398

Taksle, Beret Olsdatter, I:437

Tallaksen, Salve, I:74

Tamnes, Christen Jokumsen, I:222

Tangen, Ellev Bjørnsen. *See*
Bjørnsen, Ellev

Tarladsen, Lars, III:127

Tarladsen, Sigri, III:127

Tarldsen, Guttorm, III:127

Taxdahl, Ole J. *See* Taksdal, Ole
Jesperson

Teigen, Halvor, II:511

Teigen/Holen, Kari, II:219

Teigset, Kittil Kittilsen, I:276

Teksle, Maret/Marit, I:235, 334,
386

Teksle, Ole, I:334, 366

Teksle, Sjul Olsen, I:386

Tellefsen, Aasine, III:163

Tellefsen, Tellef J., III:163

Terkildsen, Edvard, II:88

Torvetjern/Torvetjønn, Aanund/
  Anund Olsen, II:302, 303, 523;
  III:238, 239, 572–573
Torvetjern/Torvetjønn, Gisle,
  II:539, 540
Torvetjern/Torvetjønn, Gro
  Olsdatter, II:302, 539–540;
  III:494–495, 542–543, 564–
  565, 572–573, 578–579
Torvetjern/Torvetjønn, Nels/Nils
  Olsen. See Olsen/Olson Nels/
  Nils Torvetjønn
Torvetjern/Torvetjønn, Ole Olsen,
  II:202, 523; III:548
Tosholm, Anders, II:225
Tosholm, Anton, II:225
Tostenrud, Knud, I:142
Tostensdatter, Rønnaug, III:173,
  213
Towning. See Tonning
Traasdahl, Jakob Olsen, III:171,
  173
Tretterud, Knut, I:317
Trintrud, Knut, II:51
Trodal, Ole, III:172
Trollerud, Kjersti, I:397–398
Trollerud, Lars, I:322
Tronsen/Thronsen, Mrs., III:163
Tronsgaard, O. T., III:166
Trovatn, Ole Knutsen, I:83, 84
Trumpy, James, I:92, 111, 343,
  345
Tryhus, Endre Tomassen, I:64, 66
Tufte, Halvor Endresen, I:265
Tufte, Hermod Nilsen, I:64, 66
Tufte, Kari, I:66
Tufte, Nils, I:66
Tufte, Sigrid, I:66
Tufto, Halvor Endresen, I:244
Tufto, Hermod, I:154
Tullerud, Anne, I:333

Tunga. See Tonga/Tunga
Turkeknut, Mr., III:129
Turkeknut, Mrs., III:129
Turmo, Andreas, II:358
Tvede, Elise. See Wærenskjold,
  Elise Tvede
Tvedt, Lars, II:404–405; II:404–
  405, 511
Tveito, Hans Torgrimsen, I:98
Tveter, Hans Iverson, II:270, 289,
  331–32
Tøndevold, Gunder, II:473
Tønnesen, Ole, III:166–167
Tønnesen, Thora/Tulla/Tulle,
  III:164–165, 166–167
Tørrisdatter, Eva, I:236, 239
Tørrisen/Tørrissen, Christen,
  I:238
Tørrisen/Tørrissen, Kirsti
  Olsdatter, I:238, 239
Tørrisen/Tørrissen, Peder, I:236,
  239

Ubø, Anders, I:216
Udgaard, Ole, III:87
Ulen, Anne, III:229
Ulen, Ole Haraldsen, I:434, 435
Ulgenes, Jacob, III:296
Ullensvang, Rasmus, III:304
Ulshagen, Anders, III:176, 183
Ulshagen, Ingebjørg/Ingeborg,
  II:530; III:183, 199, 223
Ulshagen, Thor/Tor Torsen,
  II:530; III:176, 177, 183, 199,
  205, 206, 215
Ulsness/Ulsnæss/Ulnes, Halvor
  Hansen, II:378–379, 439–440,
  510–511, 546–547
Ulsness/Ulsnæss/Ulnes, Margit/
  Magrit, II:378, 511
Ulveholen, Marie, II:219

Ulvin, Ludvig, III:457
Ulvin, Ole, III:457
Undene, Sven, I:297
Urheim, Jakob/Jacob Larsen,
    II:264, 265, 323, 404, 525–
    526; III:296–297, 305–306,
    327–328, 351–352
Urheim, Lars Jakobsen, II:526
Urheim, Lars Larsen, II:321, 322,
    405, 525, 526
Urheim, Lena, III:306
Urheim, Oddmund, II:405
Urheim, Samson, J., III:327
Urheim, Torsten/Torstein, II:404,
    525, 526
Ursin, Jens Herlef, II:207–208,
    366–367, 383–384, 409–410
Utheim, Lars Larsen, II:264–265
Utne, Torbjørg, II:497

Vahl, Mr., I:77
Valde, Andreas, III:568
Valde, Karole, III:535
Valeur, Peter, I:53, 55
Valle, Albert Johnsen, III:567
Valle, Beret, III:388
Valle, Dr., II:182
Valseth, K. A., III:423
Vammen, Torkel Olsen, I:154
Vanderbilt, William Henry, II:374
Vangberg, A., III:509
Vangen, B., II:531
Vangen, Berit, III:108
Vangen, Johan, III:262–263
Vangen, Marit, II:500
Vangestad, Ole Nirisen, I:177, 179
Vasbraavollen, Christin, I:351, 352
Vatland, Lars, III:350
Vatland, Ole, III:359
Vatland, Samuel Samuelsen,
    III:365, 413, 519

Vatland, Sofie. See Erfjord, Sofie
Vatland, Svend Samuelsen,
    III:349–350, 358–359,
    364–365, 371, 411–412, 518,
    620–621
Vatland, Torberg Torkelsdatter,
    III:365
Vatland, Torkel Samuelsen, III:413
Vatnebrønn, Gullik Sjursen, I:179
Veen, Matias, III:328, 330
Veggar, Ole, I:234, 235
Vehus, A., I:146
Vehus, Halvor, I:83–84
Vehus, Jørgen, I:149
Velta, Haagen, II:423
Vermunsen, Johannes, I:347
Veslegard, Birgit Mikkelsdatter,
    I:286, 287
Veslehaugen, Tosten Mikkelsen,
    III:129, 131
Vestergaard, Ole, III:521
Vesthagen, Ole Arild, I:352
Vethammer/Vethamer, Ole. See
    Hammer, Ole
Viberg, Mr., I:127–128
Victoria, Queen, I:250
Vig, Ole, III:331, 332, 337, 520
Vig, Sjur, II:75
Vigenstad, Ole Torstensen/
    Torstensensen, I:403, 415, 462,
    463, 465, 466; II:54, 65–66,
    83, 84
Vigenstad, Paul Torstensen, I:404,
    405, 466; II:29, 35–36, 54–55,
    61, 65–66, 85–86
Vigenstad, Simen Torstensen,
    II:27, 83, 84, 85
Vigenstad, Tor/Thor Torstensen,
    I:404–405, 418, 462–465, 466;
    II:27–28, 29, 35–36, 54–55, 61,
    83, 84, 85–86

Vigenstad, Tosten, I:214
Viger, Hans N., II:72, 73, 225
Viger, Maren, II:72, 73
Viger, Marie, II:225
Viger, Ole, I:266, 280; II:225
Vigerus. *See* Vigerust
Vigerust, Jacob/Jakob, II:103–104
Vigerust, Jakob Bjørnersen, II:458
Vigerust, Jakob Olson, II:367–368
Vigerust, Marie Olsdatter/Mari,
     II:323, 325, 344–345, 429, 431,
     455–456, 477, 479, 528, 537–
     538, 542, 548–549, 553–554;
     III:64–65, 138, 139, 140, 150,
     151, 186, 187, 188–189, 191,
     229, 251–252
Vigerust, Ole Olsen, II:103–104,
     367–368, 429, 430
Vigerust, Ragnhild Jakobsdatter,
     II:103–104, 345, 367–368, 457;
     III:150
Vigerust, Ragnhild Olsdatter,
     II:538, 543–544. *See also*
     Olson, Rena/Ragnhild
Vik, Anders, I:55
Vik, Andrea Marie, III:148
Vik, Gina, III:149–150
Vik, Johannes Ommundsen, I:55
Vik, Jørgina Gustava, III:150
Vik, Kristian Terjesen, III:148, 150
Vik, Mr., III:589
Vik, Sevat Olsen, II:421, 423,
     475–476; III:194–195
Vike, Dordei Knutsdatter, I:298–
     299, 311–312, 453
Vike, Gulleik/Gullik Ivarson,
     I:298, 299, 312
Vike, Knud Ivarson, I:298–299,
     311–312
Vike, Kristofer Sundsdal, III:126

Vike, Styrk, I:299
Viker, Nils Hansen, I:231, 232,
     233, 289
Viker, Ole, I:289
Vikermoen, Kari, III:413
Vikingstad, Nils Johannes, III:184,
     185
Vinger, Torger, I:167
Vingestad, Tosten, I:214
Vinje, Aasmund Olavsson, III:420,
     421
Vinne, Olaus, II:294
Vinzent, Charles, II:38, 39
Vinzent, Lina (Caroline Amalie),
     I:94; II:37, 39
Vinzent, Mads, I:89, 94, 147
Virak, Christian, I:393
Virak, Erik Asbjørnsen, I:393, 394
Virak, Ingebor Sofie, I:393
Virak, Siri Gabrielsdatter, I:394;
     II:113–114
Vitberg, Marie/Mari, III:338, 588
Vogtvedt, Gunder, I:437
Voldslien, Ole, I:105
Vold/Wold, Anne, II:91
Vold/Wold, Elling Ellingsen,
     I:292, 310–311, 314–315, 318,
     418–419, 445; II:91; II:215,
     306–307, 310
Vold/Wold, Erik Tidemansen,
     II:312, 314
Vold/Wold, Gina, III:291
Vold/Wold, Johanna, III:272, 282
Vold/Wold, John, II:214; III:266,
     275, 281
Vold/Wold, Kristian, III:529
Vold/Wold, Lars, III:291–292

Wærenskjold, Niels, I:344–345,
356, 449; II:88, 295, 296, 297,
308, 339, 397, 424, 425, 452,
454, 498, 502–503, 504, 533,
552; III:71, 93, 95, 100
Wærenskjold, Ophelia, II:37, 347
Wærenskjold, Otto, I:149, 344–
345, 356, 449; II:37, 38, 88, 89,
296, 308, 339, 346, 347, 397,
424, 452, 498, 503, 533, 552;
III:70, 71, 93, 95, 99–100, 111,
112
Wærenskjold, Thorvald August
(Tulle), I:246, 345, 353–354,
356, 375, 409, 449; II:89

Yerkes, Charles, III:306
Ylvisaker, Niels Thorbjørnsen,
II:47, 48
Ystaas, Iver Sjursen, II:93–94,
107–108, 120–121, 196; III:507
Ystanes/Estanes, Johannes Ossden.
See Estnes, John
Ystanes/Ovstanes, Jacob
Mikkelsen, III:448, 449
Ytterhus, Berit, III:266

Zahl, E. B. Kjerschow/Kjerskov/
Kjerskow, II:138, 207–208,
366–367, 383–384, 409–410,
456–457; III:69, 74–75, 78,
79–80, 135–136, 191–192, 294,
308, 580
Ziener, Mr., I:108

Ødeberg, Gullik, II:374
Ødegaard. See also Solem

Ødegaard, Amalie, II:389–390,
412–413, 427, 442, 443, 461–
462, 490–491, 509, 511, 534,
540, 541, 560; III:61, 62, 114,
132, 219, 220, 258, 340–341,
342, 475–476, 478
Ødegaard, Borghild, III:341,
526–527
Ødegaard, Karen Olsdatter,
II:355–356, 379–380
Ødegaard, Marie Kristoffersdatter,
III:248–249
Ødegaard, Ole Tobias Olsen,
II:320–321, 355–356, 389–390,
412–413, 427, 442, 461–462,
507, 534, 540, 560, 561; III:61,
62, 114, 183, 196, 219, 475–
476
Øien, Lars, II:29
Øina, Berruld/Beruld, I:70, 74
Økri, Jens Larsen, I:302
Øksendal, Nils Tobias Pedersen,
I:347
Ørbæk, Andreas, I:109, 112, 147
Ørbæk, Andreas H., I:248
Ørbæk, Gina, I:248
Ørbæk, Mrs., III:94
Ørbæk, Ole Johan, I:247, 248,
376, 410; II:37, 38, 39; III:94,
96
Ørbæk, Ouline. See Reiersen,
Ouline
Ørbæk, Sigurd, I:246–247, 248,
357, 376; II:39, 346, 347, 426,
453
Ørsteen, Ole Toresen, I:396
Ørstein, Ingebjørg Gulliksdatter,
III:313–314, 491
Ørstein, Ingebjørg Hansdatter,
III:490–491, 525–526, 541–542
Ørstein, Knut Olsen, I:398; III:314

Ørstein, Ole Olsen, I:179
Ørsten, Knut, I:250
Østensen, Andreas, II:206
Østensen, Jens, III:284
Østern, Andrine, I:258, 301–302
Østern, Carl, I:122, 159–160, 181, 196, 197
Østern, Caroline, I:256
Østern, Christen, I:123, 160, 182, 195–196, 257, 258
Østern, Christine Engebretsdatter, I:120, 122, 123, 163, 165, 195, 258
Østern, Engebret Jacobsen, I:159–160, 165, 197, 256
Østern, Gullik Olsen, I:123, 160, 162, 163, 164, 165, 181–182, 195–196, 197, 258, 300, 302
Østern, Haagine Engebretsdatter, I:195
Østern, Helga Pauline, I:181, 256
Østern, Ingebret, I:122
Østern, Jacob Engebretsen, I:120, 123, 160, 161, 165, 256, 302
Østern, Jacob/Jakob Olsen, I:120–121, 123, 159, 161–162, 164–165, 180, 197, 256, 257, 258, 302
Østern, John, I:302
Østern, Karen Elise, I:301
Østern, Karen Engebretsdatter, I:161, 162, 163, 165, 181, 182
Østern, Lars, I:122, 159–160, 181, 196, 197, 257, 302
Østern, Laurine Olsdatter, I:120, 123. See also Eeg, Laurine
Østern, Maren Christine, I:301
Østern, Martine, I:197, 258
Østern, Olava, I:181, 182
Østern, Olof, I:163, 195
Østern, Torine/Thorine, I:197, 258

Østerneie/Østerneiet, I:258, 302
Østhagen. See Easthagen
Østhus, Elisabeth Maria, I:237
Østrem, Torkel Didriksen, I:414
Øverby, Gulbraand/Gulbrand, II:285; III:571
Øverland, Hans Andreas Martin Hansen, I:217
Øverland, Hans Ormsen, I:215, 217
Øverland, O. A., III:70, 72
Øvjord, Erik, III:104–105
Øxendal, Hans, II:55, 113
Øxendal, Ingeborg, II:482
Øxendal, Olene, I:393
Øygarden, Haldis Tolleivsdatter Opsata, II:327
Øymoen, Endre Gulbrandsen, I:232

sects, I:61–62, 174, 207, 211–
212, 284, 293–294, 347,
371, 446–447, 452; II:84,
118, 169–170, 189, 406;
III:119–120, 362, 505, 519
See also religion; specific
denominations
*Church Monthly Times (Kirkelig
Maanedstidende)*, I:255, 466;
II:56, 75, 83, 85, 94, 95
*The Church Times (Kirkelig
Tidende)*, I:253–254; II:255;
III:81, 82
Civil War, U.S. (1861–1865),
I:282, 286, 294, 289, 291,
293, 295–297, 298, 299, 300,
304–305, 306, 307, 321, 323,
324–325, 336, 381; III:510–512
class differences, I:92, 93, 122,
150, 164, 366, 398; II:39, 108,
233, 265, 269, 448; III:241,
404, 456, 465, 545
climate, I:50, 71, 90, 102, 110,
150, 189, 196, 201, 205, 221,
227, 232, 243, 461, 465; II:52,
66, 90, 93, 110, 108, 121, 160,
172, 183, 187, 198, 204, 205,
232, 245, 263, 289, 280, 341,
346, 354, 360, 365, 366, 386,
440–441, 459, 461, 501, 518,
545, 552; III:64, 89, 118, 123,
138–139, 177, 180, 184, 195–
196, 204, 208, 283, 320, 340,
361, 404, 407, 447, 454, 502–
503, 544, 553, 588, 599, 607
clothing
cost of, I:51, 124, 281–282,
324, 438; III:532–533
woolen, I:51, 72, 91, 161, 164,
194, 238–239, 261, 346, 392;
II:408, 416, 505, 515, 528;
III:272

cold fever. *See* ague
The Commander's Daughters
(Lie), II:425, 426
confirmation, rite of, I:208, 214,
215, 420, 426, 452, 454; II:50,
60, 102, 130, 141, 148, 167,
201, 215, 376, 377, 391, 394,
406, 443, 547; III:129, 193,
197, 238, 260, 376, 526
consumption. *See* tuberculosis
Crimean War (1853–1856), I:193
crofter. *See husmann/
hussmannsplas*
crops
damaged, I:289, 402, 409, 419;
II:64, 111, 116, 120, 134,
183, 188–189, 193, 195, 196,
201, 211, 220, 275, 357, 374,
396, 413, 414–415, 430,
462–463, 474, 475, 476–
477, 484, 513, 535–536,
545; III:179, 194, 221, 183,
277–278, 344, 348, 409,
494, 515, 524, 534, 539,
547–548, 561, 625
harvest yields, I:67, 83, 107,
178, 234, 244, 256, 276–
277, 328, 385, 392, 395,
426–427, 459; II:52–53, 62,
70, 81, 96, 99, 102, 112,
140, 147, 152, 167, 183, 189,
196, 208–209, 211, 214,
221–222, 264, 287, 299,
342, 364, 376–377, 406,
423, 433, 484, 507, 535–
536, 547; III:194, 199, 220,
245, 278, 336, 346, 373,
381, 406, 442, 445, 482,
524, 561, 568, 571, 588,
589, 609, 623–624

prices, I:236–237, 242, 268, 276–277, 377, 391, 426, 436–437, 439, 459, 461; II:60, 102, 133, 172–173, 186, 196, 211, 322–323, 342–343, 348–349, 363, 376–377, 479, 518; III:100, 139, 171, 188, 207, 278, 349, 361, 373, 439, 454, 468, 471, 502, 507, 524, 568, 609

sharecropping, II:34, 72, 147, 482, 492; III:125, 147, 286, 298, 406, 454, 517

types, I:86–87, 90–91, 99, 107, 155, 178, 327, 380, 436; II:35, 43, 124, 145, 153, 191, 209, 303, 334, 342, 374; III:100, 133, 193, 257, 320, 447, 471, 490, 541, 561, 580

death, I:76–78, 87, 100–101, 104, 113, 115, 117, 118, 132, 145, 147–149, 157, 229, 232, 308, 316, 353, 356, 395, 441–442, 450, 453; II:25–26, 69, 74, 79, 82, 88–89, 91–92, 109, 124, 136, 150, 158–159, 243–244, 427, 246–247, 282, 372, 375, 427–428, 440–441, 501, 502; III:94, 111–112, 112–113, 118–119, 148–149, 184, 206, 209, 213, 241, 249, 251, 254, 269–270, 305, 383–384, 390, 395–396, 402–403, 408–409, 413, 423–424, 434–435, 442, 454, 472, 475–476, 484–485, 504–506, 516, 531, 563–564, 573, 584

debt. *See under* money

Decorah Posten (newspaper), III:110, 346, 556

deer and game, I:164, 205, 221

Democratic Party, II:292, 321; III:100, 103, 106, 119, 122, 174, 264, 339, 557, 558

diarrhea, I:136, 145, 157, 164, 298, 409; II:463, 481; III:538, 610–611

The Diary of Elisabeth Koren, III:507

diphtheria, II:463, 481; III:115, 538

disease

in Civil War, I:344

epidemics, I:52, 59, 61, 75, 82, 132, 123, 136, 147–150, 157, 189; II:43, 58, 487; III:230

land quality and, I:50, 52

medicine, I:71, 77, 81, 88, 95, 144, 145, 147–148, 149, 174, 185, 361

recovery from, I:47, 49–50, 80–81

See also specific diseases

The District Governor's Daughters (Collett), II:425, 426

A Doll's House (Ibsen), II:308, 309

Duluth Skandinav (newspaper), II:278

dysentery, I:131, 136, 147, 148, 150; II:44

education

English schools (public school), I:178–179, 237, 245, 276, 335, 337, 339, 386, 423, 426, 452, 460, 465; II:32, 78, 108, 135, 148, 171, 214, 215, 245, 254–255, 334, 341, 349, 355, 366, 367–368, 510, 515, 538, 557; III:79, 115, 134, 187, 218, 221, 223, 341, 481–482, 432, 533, 548

good, I:48, 52; II:316

modest, I:79, 262

Norwegian schools (parochial school), I:237, 245, 276, 337, 378, 426, 460, 465; II:76, 137, 334, 337, 355; III:134, 187, 197, 221, 273, 341

prosperity and, I:464

school locations, I:52, 237; II:60, 66

teaching, I:53, 82, 335, 337, 423, 462; II:28, 29, 66, 84, 212, 328–330, 438, 521; III:79, 185, 197, 218, 256, 273, 335, 358, 364, 491–492, 509, 588

Eielsen Synod, II:46, 48, 169, 180. *See also* Norwegian Evangelical Lutheran synod

Elling synod, I:452; II:33, 46, 169. *See also* Norwegian Evangelical Lutheran synod

Emigranten (newspaper), I:275, 337, 352, 357

emigration

advice for, I:49, 51–52, 54, 55, 62, 65, 69, 72–73, 78, 83, 85–86, 91, 97, 98, 104, 106, 124, 152, 162–163, 170, 176, 185, 204, 268–269, 270, 277, 291–292, 351, 379, 388–389, 394, 404–405, 459–460; II:40, 58, 76–77, 116–117, 177, 255–257, 262, 274, 303, 304, 486, 516, 528; III:130, 154–155, 170, 190, 295, 301–302, 304–305, 369–370

anti-, I:49

cost of, I:72, 91, 122; II:154, 206, 297, 310, 443, 470, 486, 539; III:62, 78, 400, 417, 422, 529

customs inspections, I:346, 348, 363

inland travel, I:63–64, 80, 92, 111, 113, 120, 127–138, 153–155, 158, 163, 166, 189, 190–191, 193, 208–209, 228, 249, 278–279, 346, 360–362, 372, 391, 392, 408; II:49, 56, 67–68, 71–73, 93, 98, 203, 228, 239–240, 248, 296, 318, 392, 494–495, 529; III:95, 98, 261, 382–383, 457

prepaid tickets for farm workers, I:427–428; II:60, 134, 259, 283, 287, 297, 432, 433; III:61–62

return to homeland, I:49, 50, 58, 78, 82, 84, 105, 217, 231–232, 275, 288–289, 375, 379, 428, 448; II:82, 87, 92, 130, 138, 141, 142, 145, 156, 188, 207–208, 291, 303, 304–305, 359, 371, 411, 433, 532, 538, 543, 548; III:64–65, 71, 75, 138, 160, 169, 171, 174, 206, 275, 328, 362, 392, 400, 420, 428, 440, 441, 457, 461, 465, 598, 625–626

trans-Atlantic travel, I:53, 56, 61, 63, 68–69, 96, 106, 111, 121–122, 124, 127, 140–142, 151–152, 189, 203–204, 228–229, 268–269, 310, 341, 346, 350–351, 363, 403, 424; II:67, 68, 160–163, 192, 202–203, 235–239, 240, 241, 248, 251, 271–272, 274, 338, 355–356, 487, 489–490, 493–494, 526–527; III:63, 136–137, 239–240, 264–267, 308–312, 417, 456–457, 514, 522, 540–541, 622

Hauge synod, II:33, 169, 180, 445; III:350, 359, 362, 519. *See also* Norwegian Evangelical Lutheran synod

health. *See* disease

Homestead Act (1862), I:200, 309, 444, 445, 463; II:64, 379, 547

housing quality, I:65, 191, 430; II:191–192, 210, 253, 435, 478; III:410

husmann/hussmannsplas, I:197, 359, 366, 379, 398; II:42, 58, 127, 180; III:303

illness. *See* disease; specific diseases

Illustreret Ugeblad (publication), II:425, 426

Indians, I:64, 125–126, 130, 133, 137, 279, 313, 315, 321, 328, 331, 376, 382, 388, 408, 414, 432; II:49, 72, 124–125, 166, 253, 260, 266–267, 512, 513, 514, 518–519; III:209, 307, 357

influenza, II:483, 487, 540, 542, 544, 545; III:87, 113, 152, 165, 226, 230, 427, 572–573

inheritance, I:101, 122, 125, 166, 170, 194, 210, 244–245, 258, 286, 292, 305, 315, 318, 330, 375–376, 397–398, 445, 447, 466, 468; II:25, 59, 139, 142, 159, 218, 227, 349, 466, 551; III:141, 151–152, 282, 428, 445, 473, 491, 493, 496, 529, 542, 617, 621. *See also* allodial rights

"Intruders on Native Ground" (Øverland), II:263

The Jungle (Sinclair), III:545–546

King Midas (Heiberg), II:498, 499

Kirkelig Maanedstidende (Church Monthly Times), I:255, 466; II:56, 75, 83, 85, 94, 95

Kirkelig Tidende (Church Times), I:253–254, 255; II:101; III:81, 82

labor. *See* employment

Læsebog for Børn (Nilsen), III:146

La Grippe. *See* influenza

land

congress, I:106, 108, 161–162, 249, 413

cost of, I:47, 49, 51, 58–59, 64, 71, 73, 102, 106–107, 110, 121, 155–156, 161, 162, 178, 189, 222, 225, 227, 235, 261, 268, 331, 369, 413, 430, 461; II:40, 45, 49, 102, 133, 165, 171, 176, 181, 253, 260–261, 281, 286, 295, 333, 342, 364, 450, 456–457, 472; III:207, 232, 237, 246, 256, 290, 360, 447, 471, 503, 539, 542, 564

disease and, I:52

forest, I:51, 59, 64, 71, 85, 163, 192, 221, 225, 232, 249, 269, 293, 321, 331, 368–369, 370, 445, 461; II:49, 97–98, 125, 195, 220, 253, 342, 513; III:157, 244, 503, 547

government, I:47, 71, 73, 146, 216, 222, 225, 268, 331, 349, 388, 457, 461, 463; II:81, 96, 233, 260–261, 292, 316–317, 378–379; III:511

355, 356, 357, 367, 390, 428, 516

loneliness/longing, I:392; II:124, 126, 143, 165, 185, 266, 282, 290, 315, 318, 436, 445, 504; III:75–76, 78, 161, 187, 211, 281, 330, 448, 456, 480, 568, 594, 595, 612, 618

Louisiana Purchase Exposition (1904), III:351, 352

lumber. *See* logging; sawmills

Lutheran church, I:168, 211–212, 217, 252–255, 281, 293–294, 378–379, 420, 446–447, 452, 464; II:46, 84, 118, 169, 189, 394, 406, 509; III:90, 120, 224, 362, 372, 416, 500, 505–506. *See also* specific synods

The Lutheran Witness (journal), III:120

Luthersk Barneblad (magazine), III:146

Luthers Liv (Nilsen), III:146

Lysholm distillery, II:332

malaria, I:62, 71, 74, 82, 146–147, 164; II:183. *See also* ague

measles, I:338, 436, 454; III:115, 184, 211, 342, 576

Med blyanten (Lerche), II:309

medicine, I:71, 77, 81, 88, 95, 144, 145, 147–148, 149, 174, 185, 361

Methodist church, I:174, 206, 281, 371; II:169, 394, 406, 498, 550, 551; III:90, 92, 496, 534, 535

Mexican-American War (1846–1848), I:83

A Midsummer Night's Dream (Shakespeare), III:583

military draft, I:104, 305, 309,

319–320, 321, 323, 325, 327, 329, 332–333

mills, I:82, 87, 90, 92, 103, 159, 309; II:41, 70, 85, 180, 207, 527, 554; III:174. *See also* sawmills

Milwaukee and Mississippi Railroad, I:269

Minneapolis Tidende (newspaper), III:110, 204, 225, 346

Minnesota (newspaper), II:278

Missouri synod, II:51, 77, 84, 86

money
    currencies, I:55, 72, 99, 107, 153, 227, 329, 339, 384; II:87, 138
    debt, I:87, 113, 174, 233, 257, 301, 314, 326, 334, 379, 385, 388, 395, 425, 427, 430, 439, 445, 465–466; II:62, 74–75, 179, 204, 206, 207, 248, 286, 296, 303, 339, 366–367, 382, 383, 410–411, 412, 423, 424–425, 432, 436, 481, 484, 513–514, 547; III:71, 93, 100, 135–136, 152, 172, 241, 256, 277, 366, 377, 381–382, 392, 399, 400, 477, 511, 578, 580, 591
    interest rates, I:121, 213, 231–232, 249, 268, 300, 377, 395, 445, 447, 459; III:57–58, 78, 133, 139, 172, 196, 220, 292, 317, 397, 424, 457, 492, 503, 533; III:74, 78, 93, 399, 400, 454, 529, 574, 578, 580
    transfers, I:245, 314, 315–316; II:130, 157; III:74, 78, 102, 148, 153, 166, 178, 205, 213, 298, 324, 381, 392, 395, 399, 423, 549, 560, 577–578, 600, 604
    value of, I:60, 87, 97, 138; II:138

Morgenbladet (newspaper), I:53,
55, 104, 146, 187, 248; III:112,
113
Mormons, I:134, 187; II:406
mosquitoes, I:72, 417; II:145;
III:498

names, family. *See* patronymics
Native Americans. *See* Indians
nervous fever. *See* typhoid
newspapers, Norwegian, I:55,
340, 351–352; II:278, 479. *See
also* specific newspapers
Norden (Relling), II:309
Nordenfjeldske Tidende
(newspaper), II:471
Nordlyset (newspaper), II:277, 278
Nordmands-forbundet 27
(magazine), I:80
Nordstjernen (newspaper), II:277,
278
Nordvesten (newspaper), II:277,
278
Norge og Amerika (newsletter),
I:93
Norges Sjøfartstidende
(newspaper), III:70, 71
Norma Holm og andre skildringer
(Straaberg), III:326
Northern Pacific Railroad, II:209
Norway and America (newsletter),
I:93
Norwegian Evangelical Lutheran
synod, I:168, 171, 211, 234–
235, 254, 452; II:33, 46, 51,
77, 86, 118, 137, 168, 169, 180,
189, 403, 558; III:119–120,
122, 339, 341, 362, 474, 505,
506, 507, 543, 604, 615
Norwegian Lutheran Church
of America, III:615. *See also*

United Lutheran Church in
America
Nylænde (journal), II:453, 454

Ohio synod, II:86
On the Paths of God (Bjørnson),
II:498, 499

Panic of 1893, III:80–81, 85, 86,
90
Paris Commune, II:40
passports, I:289–290
pastoral care. *See under* religion
patronymics, I:84, 166, 180, 342,
369–370, 382, 384; II:42, 104,
130, 146, 321, 371, 413, 418,
451, 528; III:82, 191, 235
People's Party (Populists), III:76,
100, 104, 106, 122
Philadelphia and Reading
Railroad, II:332–333
Philippine-American War (1899–
1902), III:231, 280, 329
photographs. *See* portraits
pleurisy, III:343
pneumonia, I:247; II:481; III:115,
364, 438
politics, U.S., I:401, 427, 464;
II:62, 278, 292, 317; III:99–
100, 103–104, 105–106, 119,
169, 174, 208, 220, 288–289,
332–334, 348, 449–450, 557,
596. *See also* specific parties
Populists. *See* People's Party
(Populists)
portraits, I:247, 272, 312, 317,
343, 351, 353, 355, 357, 358,
372, 375, 409, 410, 411, 419,
437–438, 448, 449, 454–455,
467; II:28, 37, 45, 65, 76, 82,
103, 111, 113, 115, 126, 130,

136, 144–145, 149, 156, 157,
166, 175, 177, 184, 193–194,
197, 198, 202, 220, 227,
276–277, 284, 295, 332, 337,
345, 351, 355, 356, 373, 399,
410, 451, 470, 471, 482, 507,
512, 513, 515, 522, 536, 558,
560–561; III:66, 70, 87, 117,
123–124, 143, 175, 182, 198,
202, 207, 219, 223, 234, 236,
253, 254, 270, 282, 286–287,
314, 363, 365, 370, 374, 383,
386, 397, 405, 416, 437, 441,
443, 474, 481, 483, 497, 517–
518, 522–523, 524, 539, 546,
571–572, 585, 601, 607, 624

postage
cost of, I:54–55, 58, 60, 65, 67,
68, 70, 75, 98, 102, 157, 179,
194, 200, 228, 235, 238,
286, 313, 355, 391, 394, 448
scams, I:305, 313, 394, 448

Posten (newspaper), II:453, 454

poverty committee, I:439, 440–
441

precentors, II:123, 170, 212, 273,
329, 331; III:129, 134, 462–
464, 612

Preemption Act (1830), I:49,
158–159, 200

Presbyterian church, I:281

*Professorene Oftedal og
Weenaas's "Wisconsinisme"
betragtet i Sandhedens Lys*
(Preus), II:132

Progressive Party, III:558

prohibitionists, III:90, 104, 106

Prohibition Party, III:106, 122

Psalme-Bog (Høegh-Guldberg),
I:69, 70, 187, 199, 200, 239;
II:171

Quakers, I:206

quinine, I:144, 147–149

railroad
employment, I:167, 331, 425;
II:35, 36, 43, 72, 180, 205,
305, 337, 419, 527, 548;
III:65, 80, 424, 469
expansion of, I:193, 222, 276,
331, 365, 388, 430, 434, 444,
456; II:41, 186, 205, 224,
259, 260, 305, 318, 336, 341,
367, 399–400; III:110, 192,
246, 256, 360, 492, 513, 551,
609
land, I:249, 268, 445; II:220,
223, 292, 316–317, 342,
399–400
as mode of travel, I:124, 167,
189, 193, 228, 243, 256, 276,
338, 360, 363–364, 389, 408,
456; II:46, 67, 260, 263, 296,
318, 367, 494–495; III:95,
323, 450

Red River Posten (newspaper),
II:277, 278

Red River Tidende (newspaper),
II:277, 278

religion
freedom of, I:237, 281, 378;
II:76; III:230, 231, 332, 334,
500
observing, I:104, 156–157, 168–
169, 199–200, 229, 269, 289,
347, 349, 451, 464; II:30,
118, 119, 168, 325, 329, 359,
380–382, 386, 394–396, 419,
480, 496–497; III:140–141,
371–372, 495, 547

pastoral care, I:49, 178–179, 222, 237, 246, 252, 284, 335, 380; II:31–33, 38, 66, 76, 96, 134–135, 137, 142, 186, 189, 212, 247, 273, 282, 327, 394, 402, 427–428, 441; III:180, 234, 336, 358

See also churches; specific denominations

Republican Party, II:292; III:86, 103, 104, 106, 119, 122, 143, 174, 261, 339, 442, 558, 596

rheumatic fever, III:617

Rjukan Dagblad (newspaper), I:82

Russo-Japanese War (1904–1905), III:344, 348–349

Russo-Turkish War (1877–1878), II:173

Salmebog for Lutherske Kristne i America, III:121, 145

En Saloonkeepers Datter (Janson), II:425, 426

sawmills, I:103, 159; II:85, 88, 316, 324, 361, 456, 471, 486, 495, 526; III:69, 79, 128, 283, 313, 400, 469–470, 537, 616

Scandinavian Augustana synod, I:255

Scandinavian Nature and Society (Heggtveit), II:498, 499

scarlet fever, III:269, 309, 371, 538

schools. *See* education

seasickness, I:50, 63, 78, 140–141, 184, 363

A Selection of Poetry and Prose from the Writings of Various Authors, II:498, 499

settlements, Norwegian, I:60, 62, 82, 89–90, 109–111, 117–118, 121, 123, 143, 145, 148, 150,
168–169, 171, 200, 247, 262, 326, 376, 382, 403, 408, 411–412; II:46, 66, 105, 113, 308, 398; III:236, 383

sharecropping. *See under* crops

shoemaker trade, I:105, 167, 440; II:44, 48, 96, 129, 164, 166, 176, 178, 223, 257, 261, 268, 274, 304–305, 332, 353, 369–370; III:313, 467–468

sickness. *See* disease

silver prospecting, I:53, 400, 401, 432; II:260, 268

Sioux Line Railroad, III:322, 360, 368, 370, 371

Skandinaven (newspaper), II:355, 536, 537, 547, 560; III:61

slavery, I:48, 90, 278, 282, 291, 295, 299, 304–305, 328, 381, 420; II:92, 95

smallpox, I:113, 119

Smuler (journal), III:425

Socialist Labor Party, III:122, 339–340

Spanish-American War (1898), III:204, 208, 209, 211–212, 214, 220–221, 229, 230–231, 233

Statstidende (newspaper), III:346

Stjørdalens Blad (newspaper), III:110

St. Louis World's Fair (Louisiana Purchase Exposition, 1904), III:351, 352

St. Paul, Minneapolis, and Manitoba Railway, II:432

suffrage, I:105, 227, 278

Symra (periodical), III:507

Taale Tangen (Nilsen), III:146

taxes, I:83, 216, 259, 281, 300, 326–328, 339, 385, 388, 456; II:26, 60, 78, 137, 140–141, 187, 188, 260, 261, 292; III:86, 110, 171, 307, 392, 454, 596, 621

teaching. *See under* education

travel. *See under* emigration

Treaty of Kiel (1814), III:605, 608

True Christianity (Arndt), II:556

tuberculosis, II:51, 246; III:61, 73, 120–121, 130, 259, 414, 437, 506

Tvedestrandsposten (newspaper), III:367

typhoid, I:95; II:59, 376, 517; III:83, 84, 222, 224, 347, 430, 431

typhus, I:89, 347; II:43, 253

Um Amerika og frendefolket I Vesterheimen (Seland), III:328

Union Pacific Railroad, III:513

United Lutheran Church in America, II:408, 509; III:106, 120, 122, 145, 173, 224, 334, 362, 543, 601

U.S.-Dakota War (1862), I:239, 321, 328–329, 331

Valdres (newspaper), III:502

Varden (journal), III:326

Verdans Gang (newspaper), I:434

Vesterheimen (newspaper), III:215, 216

Vor Tid (journal), III:328

Vossingen (newspaper), II:121

wages. *See under* employment

Washington-Posten (newspaper), III:328, 420

water quality, I:50, 64, 88, 89, 289, 309, 430; II:362; III:271–272

weather. *See* climate

West of the Great Divide (Bjork), II:263

white privilege, I:109

whooping cough, II:194–195; III:342

Wilson-Gorman Tariff Act (1894), III:86

Wisconsinismen belyst ved historiske kjendsgjerninger (Weenaas), II:132

Wisconsin synod, II:47, 86, 132

women
    employment of, I:51–52, 73, 160, 182–183, 226, 231, 347; II:114, 145, 168, 171, 452, 521; III:133, 428, 509
    forms of address, I:412
    gendered work, II:388, 418
    right to vote, III:220, 221, 602, 604
    skills of, I:392
    treatment of, I:51

World's Columbian Exhibition (1893), II:541, 551; III:62, 71

World's Fair, St. Louis. *See* St. Louis World's Fair (Louisiana Purchase Exposition, 1904)

World War I (1914–1918), III:620, 622, 624

Wounded Knee Massacre (1890), II:513

yellow fever, II:183